I AM A CHRISTIAN, BUT I HAVE QUESTIONS!

I AM A CHRISTIAN, BUT I HAVE QUESTIONS!

A JOURNEY THROUGH THE BIBLE

Dr. Darrin Berkley

New Harbor Press
Rapid City, SD

Berkley/New Harbor Press
1601 Mt Rushmore Rd, Ste 3288
Rapid City, SD 57701
www.NewHarborPress.com

I Am a Christian But I Have Questions!/Berkley. -- 1st ed.
ISBN 978-1-63357-209-6

Contents

Introduction

I am a Christian trying to meet God's expectations through trying to understand what God tells me through the Bible. In trying to increase my understanding of what God expects, it will take more than attending a two-hour church service every Sunday.

Unless I attend seminary or take theology courses in college, I may not have opportunities to assess what I have learned about Christianity. What should I do with this information? I will share it with all of you. Much of what I have learned has been taken from the *New International Version Study Bible*. This Bible has taught me more about the Word of God than any individual clergy member (pastor, minister, bishop, and so on). What I have learned can serve as a guide as to what you may learn through reading the Bible.

As one may say that trials and tribulations can be used informally to assess what you have learned from the Bible, you may always have questions about what you have learned from the Bible. Do you truly understand what you are reading? How do you appropriately apply what was done in biblical times to current times? Are messages you read literal or figurative? Do you really believe the stories in the Bible that almost seem magical, supernatural, or just impossible? Questions will arise naturally if you are trying to understand the Bible.

This book will walk through the entire Bible chapter by chapter. Each chapter will include what I learned from reading the chapter along with a question. I welcome all readers to check that what I learned is factual. It is also possible that the reader may not fully agree with what I have learned in a specific chapter due to varied interpretations. The beauty of writing this book was that I am not writing as a Bible scholar, but rather with the intention that there will be biblical dialogue between both experienced and inexperienced Christians. I would even hope that atheists, agnostics, and other faiths also reading this book would maintain dialogue about what the Bible teaches us.

All readers can gain a perspective from each chapter of the Bible through reading this book even though universal agreement on what I learned or the answers to the questions in this book may not be reached. Don't we all face this as Christians? We know very little relative to God's infinite understanding. But as Christians, we want to improve our understanding of God's expectations of us in our daily lives. It may even be possible that the Bible doesn't directly address the dilemmas we face in our lives.

However, Christians can help each other with possible answers to these questions because God has given individuals a different set of skills to build his kingdom. Through experience, God gives answers to some individuals, but not others. Who God gives answers to is not necessarily based on Christian experience, church position, age, level of education, or even intelligence. Answers to these questions may differ drastically based on personal experience and religious affiliations. Because answers to many of these questions can be subjective, again, universal agreement is unlikely to be reached.

One of the goals in writing this book is to have a dialogue about what we understand about Christianity through the Bible. Even pastors and bishops will have difficulty answering some of these questions, but they may have a broader perspective based on God's calling to preach as well as their experience listening to many people about a variety of life's challenges.

Because this dialogue is not likely to take place during a Sunday service, this book may be most useful in a Bible study. Having a variety of people in these dialogues will enrich discussions and allow listeners to set broader perspectives to the questions. All participants should be given opportunities to answer these questions to determine if some agreement can be reached. This could allow participants to make better life decisions. The size and diversity of groups can affect dialogue. Of course, this book can be read by a single individual outside of a Bible study or any church affiliation.

In conclusion, I hope readers become more curious about what is in the Bible and think about the consequences of knowing (or not knowing) the answers to these questions. I want readers to learn even more than I have learned. Additionally, it is expected that readers may want to speak with their pastors or other church leaders in a Christian church regarding the information in this book.

Why don't many Christians read the Bible if it serves as the main resource to understand how to live the Christian life? Do they believe it is necessary to read the entire Bible, or just get summaries of biblical passages by pastors, bishops, or other clergy members? Is the Bible too difficult to understand? I hope Christians will continue to work hard to learn from reading the Bible and not be afraid to ask questions to others, as well as to God through prayer. As you keep asking, God will keep supplying!

Genesis

Chapter 1
What I learned: God is an infinite being, and our finite minds can't fully understand the infinite.

The question: Does God only prefer us to eat plants although we rule over the animals?

Chapter 2
What I learned: God created man from dust; when we die, we go back to dust.

The question: Was the purpose of the tree of life to allow choice? What is the difference between temptation and allowing choices?

Chapter 3
What I learned: It is easy to excuse our sin by blaming someone else for our circumstances.

The question: How did Adam and Eve get married?

Chapter 4
What I learned: Eve's death is not mentioned in Scripture.

The question: Why was marrying relatives not a concern in Cain's day?

Chapter 5
What I learned: "Became the father of" (verse 6) may not just refer to a son, but a more distant descendant.

The question: Are the years in Adam's day (nine hundred thirty years) the same as years now? If not, what are the differences?

Chapter 6

What I learned: God gave the people one hundred twenty days to change their sinful ways.

The question: Were there other faithful people besides Noah before God destroyed the earth?

Chapter 7

What I learned: We often worry about details that we cannot control.

The question: What was the type of wickedness that made God so angry that he wiped out the face of the earth?

Chapter 8

What I learned: Every inclination of the human heart is evil from childhood.

The question: What is the significance of the freshly picked olive leaf?

Chapter 9

What I learned: Noah's three sons, Shem, Ham (the father of Canaan), and Japheth, populated the earth.

The question: Did God favor the descendants of Shem and Japheth equally?

Chapter 10

What I learned: Abraham, David, and Jesus were Shem's descendants.

The question: Is there a book in the Bible that has a family tree that lists all the names?

Chapter 11

What I learned: The tower of Babel was built for man's own greatness, not for God.

The question: What does it mean when the Bible says that "[t]he Lord came down to see the city" (verse 5)?

Chapter 12

What I learned: Even the man of faith, Abraham, lost faith when he acted in fear to deceive the Egyptians about his wife.

The question: In the days of Genesis, what was meant by the word "beautiful" to describe Sarai, Abraham's half sister and wife?

Chapter 13

What I learned: Lot, Abraham's nephew, was willing to take more land and take the risk of being near Sodom.

The question: Was it physically impossible for Abram and Lot to live together with all their assets?

Chapter 14

What I learned: Abraham gave "one-tenth" (verse 20) of captured goods to Melchizedek (a representation of Christ), which followed accepted tradition.

The question: Why were there so many wars, and was this representative of the amount of evil in that day?

Chapter 15

What I learned: A right relationship with God is based on faith—the heartfelt inner confidence that God is who he says he is and does what he says he will do.

The question: Like Abraham, why are we fearful and lack faith?

Chapter 16

What I learned: Abraham, Sarai (Abraham's wife), and Hagar (Sarai's mistress) showed a lack of faith in God's plans.

The question: Are substitute wives (custom in Abraham's day) similar to surrogates in our day?

Chapter 17

What I learned: Circumcision separated God's people from their pagan neighbors and was possibly done for health reasons.

The question: Why did God specifically change Abram's name ("exalted father") to Abraham ("father of many nations")?

Chapter 18

What I learned: Meeting another's need for food or shelter was and still is one of the most immediate and practical ways to obey God.

The question: Why does God allow nature to destroy the righteous and actions of the wicked to destroy the righteous?

Chapter 19

What I learned: Lot's two daughters had sex with him and bore two sons—Moab and Ben-Ammi, who became father of the Moabites and Ammonites (enemies of Israel).

The question: Did Lot ever realize that he impregnated both his daughters? How did he respond to this?

Chapter 20

What I learned: Abraham had a pattern of sinning (losing faith) whenever his life was in danger.

The question: Does God punish intentional and unintentional sins equally?

Chapter 21

What I learned: Sarah sent Hagar and her surrogate son, Ishmael, into the desert to fend for themselves.

The question: Why did Abimelek, Abraham's commander of forces, want to make an oath with Abraham?

Chapter 22

What I learned: Abraham's attempted sacrifice of his son was one of the greatest acts of obedience in recorded history.

The question: Does God require all Christians to be tested in order to strengthen character?

Chapter 23

What I learned: Abraham didn't use his popularity to get a deal on the purchase of property and instead paid full price.

The question: Why did Abraham choose to bury his wife, Sarah, in a foreign land?

Chapter 24

What I learned: Isaac's servant, Eliezer, looked for a wife for Isaac who had inner beauty and a servant's heart.

The question: Why did Rebekah's brother and mother want to wait ten days before letting her go with the servant?

Chapter 25

What I learned: Although Abraham had two sons, Isaac and Ishmael, he gave everything he owned to Isaac, the son born to him by Sarah (not Hagar).

The question: Did Esau understand the meaning of "birthright" (verse 31)?

Chapter 26

What I learned: Isaac lied about Rebekah being his wife, just like his father, Abraham, lied about Sarah being his wife.

The question: To best understand the Bible, how can we be sure that some people in the Bible with the same name are different people?

Chapter 27

What I learned: Although the firstborn son was entitled to the birthright, it was not actually his until the blessing was pronounced.

The question: If Isaac was hesitant about whether he was talking to Jacob or Esau, why didn't he wait to give his blessing?

Chapter 28

What I learned: Jacob made a vow and says, "[O]f all that you give me I will give you a tenth"(verse 22).

The question: Why was it acceptable practice to marry multiple wives in the earlier days (Esau)?

Chapter 29

What I learned: The Lord showed love to Leah, Jacob's first wife, by giving her children when Jacob did not.

The question: Does the number seven represent completion (number of years worked for both Rachel and Leah)?

Chapter 30

What I learned: Each of the three great patriarchs (Abraham, Isaac, and Jacob) had wives who had difficulty having children.

The question: Was there a relationship in Jacob's day between power and having children?

Chapter 31

What I learned: Laban, Rachel, and Leah's father kept small wooden or metal idols called *teraphim*.

The question: Since Leah took her father's idols, did she believe in God or the idols?

Chapter 32

What I learned: Jacob stated that he had seen God face to face, and his life was spared.

The question: Who was the "man" who wrestled with Jacob?

Chapter 33

What I learned: Esau was no longer bitter over losing his birthright and blessing when he met Jacob.

The question: Did Esau receive blessings from God through sheep, goats, and cattle?

Chapter 34

What I learned: Jacob took no action when he found out his daughter, Dinah, was raped.

The question: Did Simeon and Levi tell or force Dinah to walk alone so that she could be raped and so that they could take revenge?

Chapter 35
What I learned: Jacob's name was changed to Israel ("struggles with God").

The question: What made Reuben commit the sin of sleeping with his father's concubine, Bilhah?

Chapter 36
What I learned: Jacob and Esau were so wealthy with livestock that they could not live near each other.

The question: Why did the Bible include the family line of Esau (Edomites)?

Chapter 37
What I learned: Jacob loved Joseph more than his other sons, and Joseph bragged about it.

The question: Was Reuben a part of God's plan since he was the only son of Jacob to recommend not killing Joseph?

Chapter 38
What I learned: God expected the brothers of deceased males with no children to continue the family, and God killed Onan because he failed to do so.

The question: Why are men (such as Judah) so driven by lust when they know that it is wrong?

Chapter 39
What I learned: Others realized that God was with Joseph and gave him charge of everything they had.

The question: Why weren't the accused given the opportunities to explain themselves before they were put in prison (Joseph)?

Chapter 40
What I learned: Joseph gave God credit and gave the cupbearer a favor by interpreting his dream, but the cupbearer forgot about Joseph.

The question: Why was the baker's punishment so harsh (birds ate his flesh, and he was beheaded), but the cupbearer was released?

Chapter 41

What I learned: The wise men and magicians who were able to interpret dreams (but not Pharaoh's) had satanic powers.

The question: Do our dreams have meaningful interpretations like Pharoah's?

Chapter 42

What I learned: The dreams stated by Jacob's arrogant comments of his brothers bowing down to him came true.

The question: Why was Simeon taken from his brothers and bound while the brothers went to get Benjamin, Joseph's full brother and Jacob's youngest son?

Chapter 43

What I learned: Egyptians were not allowed to eat with Hebrews due to culture and rank.

The question: Why could Joseph's brothers not recognize his voice?

Chapter 44

What I learned: Joseph put a silver cup in his brothers' sacks to see how they would react.

The question: Why did Joseph need a silver cup to predict the future?

Chapter 45

What I learned: Pharaoh was very kind to Joseph in allowing his family to live in Egypt.

The question: What made Joseph finally give in and reveal himself to his brothers?

Chapter 46

What I learned: Once Jacob had the opportunity to see his long-lost son (Joseph), he was ready to die.

The question: Is it selfish for people to accomplish a feat, and then decide that they are ready to die?

Chapter 47

What I learned: Joseph bought the people and had control of their livestock, but was kind enough to give the people seed for food.

The question: Why did Jacob say, "[M]y years have been few and difficult" (verse 9)?

Chapter 48

What I learned: Although traditionally the firstborn received a double blessing, Jacob instead blessed the younger son, Ephraim.

The question: When Jacob told Joseph that he was about to die, did God inform him of this fact?

Chapter 49

What I learned: Jacob predicted the future for all his sons based on their actions, then he died.

The question: Why was Judah's sin (Joseph into slavery) forgiven, but Reuben's sin of sleeping with Jacob's concubine not forgiven?

Chapter 50

What I learned: Once his father died, Jacob grieved for months, then he was ready to die.

The question: What is the purpose of Jacob and Joseph being embalmed? Does this support the fact that there is truly life after death?

BOOK TWO

Exodus

Chapter 1
What I learned: The new king knew nothing about Joseph and treated the Israelites very harshly.

The question: Did Pharaoh punish the midwives for disobeying him by not killing the male babies?

Chapter 2
What I learned: Moses's mother had to hide her son because Pharaoh's law was to kill all sons of Hebrews, but then God reunited his mother with Moses.

The question: How did Moses go about killing an Egyptian and a certain number of shepherds?

Chapter 3
What I learned: Many people have experienced God in visible (but not necessarily human) form.

The question: Is it natural to experience a lack of faith as Moses did when he didn't believe he was capable to lead the Israelites out of Egypt?

Chapter 4
What I learned: The Lord was going to kill Moses because he did not get circumcised and therefore did not fulfill the conditions of God's covenant.

The question: Why did Moses need to perform signs? Why did God harden the heart of Pharaoh?

Chapter 5
What I learned: Pharaoh of Egypt had never heard of the God of Israel.

The question: Can we ever expect to understand God's timing when we are put in difficult situations?

Chapter 6

What I learned: It was difficult for Moses to send a message to Pharaoh that even the Israelites did not believe.

The question: Was it acceptable for Moses to continue to question God about the messages he was to send to Pharaoh?

Chapter 7

What I learned: The magicians and sorcerers performed the same miracles as Moses.

The question: Once the Lord plagued the Nile with blood, what did the Egyptians do to obtain water?

Chapter 8

What I learned: The plague of gnats was the first plague that the magicians could not perform; therefore, they recognized that it had to be God.

The question: Why did God decide particularly on the plagues in this order?

Chapter 9

What I learned: God confirmed that Pharaoh chose a life of resisting God when he states that he hardened Pharaoh's heart.

The question: What is the true purpose of the plagues if God knew that Pharaoh would not let the people of Israel go?

Chapter 10

What I learned: The Hebrews represented free labor for the Egyptians; therefore, Pharaoh would not let the people go.

The question: How significant was the impact of the plagues to Pharaoh?

Chapter 11

What I learned: Because of Pharaoh's stubbornness, he had already made up his mind that he would not let the Israelites go.

The question: Why did God decide upon ten plagues before allowing the Israelites to go?

Chapter 12

What I learned: Passover (allowing God to "pass over" killing the firstborn Hebrews) involved killing an innocent animal, which was equivalent to God having his innocent son killed.

The question: Why did Pharaoh want a blessing from Moses and Aaron when he never chose to listen to God?

Chapter 13

What I learned: God took the Israelites along a longer route to the promised land to avoid fighting with the Philistines and protected them as a pillar of fire and cloud.

The question: Why was it so important that the Israelites did not eat anything containing yeast?

Chapter 14

What I learned: The Israelites showed a lack of faith in God when the Egyptians pursued them.

The question: Because not one Egyptian survived, was this the primary reason why the Israelites put their trust in the Lord and in his servant, Moses?

Chapter 15

What I learned: Many of the moral laws given by God were designed to keep the Israelites free from sickness.

The question: Do we get diseases because we occasionally do not follow God's laws?

Chapter 16

What I learned: God didn't even want the Israelites to cook on the Sabbath.

The question: Did the Israelites ever grumble directly to God, or was it always directed to Moses?

Chapter 17

What I learned: The Amalekites were descendants of Esau and killed for pleasure.

The question: Were the Israelites thankful after God provided water for them?

Chapter 18

What I learned: Jethro, Moses's father-in-law, informed Moses that his burden was too heavy and to delegate his responsibilities amongst trustworthy men.

The question: Was his delegation of judges and officials equivalent to the president, employees, or volunteers?

Chapter 19

What I learned: The people of Israel were not permitted to see God in order to show that he is not like the idols of Egypt, which can be seen.

The question: Are there specific steps other than abstaining from sexual relations that were expected from God during the consecration?

Chapter 20

What I learned: Jesus gave a similar version of each of the Ten Commandments in Matthew, Mark, and Luke.

The question: Do Christians effectively follow the laws of the Sabbath and not commit adultery in their hearts?

Chapter 21

What I learned: "An eye for an eye" (verse 12) does not mean to take revenge, but rather for judges to ensure that the punishment fits the crime.

The question: Why would a slave owner not be punished for senseless violence if the slave recovered in a day or two?

Chapter 22

What I learned: The cloak was used for many things by the Israelites—one of those being collateral from a pledge since no interest should be charged.

The question: Are some laws of restitution explained here synonymous with laws of restitution used today?

Chapter 23

What I learned: The Israelites were to sow their fields and harvest for six years, then allow the poor to get food for the seventh year.

The question: What is God implying when he states, "Do not cook a young goat in its mother's milk" (verse 19)?

Chapter 24

What I learned: The sacrificing of the young bulls was proof that one life was given for another.

The question: Did Moses, Aaron, and the seventy elders truly see the God of Israel?

Chapter 25

What I learned: The offerings God received from the Israelites were gold, silver, and bronze, respectively.

The question: What factors impacted God's design of the tabernacle?

Chapter 26

What I learned: The tabernacle directions were very detailed and required the finest materials.

The question: Is there any place in the world today that has the representation of the tabernacle with all its details?

Chapter 27

What I learned: Pressed olives were used to constantly keep the lamps burning for the tabernacle.

The question: Why is it important to have the design of the altar in the Bible?

Chapter 28

What I learned: The priests used the Urim ("curses") and Thummim ("perfections") to make decisions regarding the will of God.

The question: Was appearance very important in representing honor toward God? Is this expected of worshipers today?

Chapter 29

What I learned: In the Old Testament, a priesthood was set up because a sinful person was not worthy to approach a perfect God.

The question: What was the significance of all the different offerings required by the Israelites (burnt, wave, sin, fellowship, and so on)?

Chapter 30

What I learned: The Day of Atonement was held once a year, and the high priest entered the most holy place to ask God for forgiveness.

The question: Is it expected that we will continuously sin today as it was in the Old Testament where the Israelites made temporary sacrifices?

Chapter 31

What I learned: God reminds us that without Sabbaths, we will forget the purpose for our activity and lose the balance to a faithful life.

The question: Why is little emphasis placed on the Sabbath today as compared to the times in the Old Testament?

Chapter 32

What I learned: While Moses was talking with God on the mountain, Aaron allowed the Israelites to run wild and create a golden calf.

The question: Why did God tell the Israelites to kill each other due to this situation?

Chapter 33

What I learned: Moses says, "If you are pleased with me, teach me your ways, so I may know you and continue to find favor with you"(verse 13).

The question: Why does it say in verse 11 that Moses was spoken to face to face, but in verse 20 it says that no one can see God's face and live?

Chapter 34

What I learned: The Festival of Ingathering requires that all men meet with God three times a year.

The question: What was the purpose of the veil that Moses removed when talking to God and used to cover his face when with the Israelites?

Chapter 35

What I learned: Key tabernacle pieces were symbolic between God and his people.

The question: How do we best use our job-related skills to strengthen God's kingdom?

Chapter 36

What I learned: A lot of skilled workers as well as help from fellow Israelites were necessary to build the tabernacle.

The question: Why does the Bible not include visual representations of the building of the tabernacle as well as other events?

Chapter 37

What I learned: The ark was Israel's most sacred object and was kept in the most holy place in the tabernacle.

The question: Is the ark still in existence today?

Chapter 38

What I learned: Aaron's son, Ithamar, was responsible for building the tabernacle.

The question: Is the plan for the design of the tabernacle beyond human understanding?

Chapter 39

What I learned: God and Moses were pleased with all of the details and design of the tabernacle by the Israelites, and Moses blessed them.

The question: Is there a possibility that the Israelites encountered complications throughout the design of the tabernacle?

Chapter 40

What I learned: The tabernacle was God's home on earth.
The question: What was involved in the consecration process?

BOOK THREE

Leviticus

Chapter 1
What I learned: During animal sacrifice, a person laid a hand on the head of the animal to symbolize complete identification with the animal as a substitute.

The question: Why were some sacrifices voluntary, while others were required?

Chapter 2
What I learned: Yeast grows in bread dough, is a bacterial fungus, and affects the loaf just as sin affects a person's life.

The question: Is the salt (representative of penetrating, preserving, and aiding in life) equivalent to salt used today?

Chapter 3
What I learned: A person was permitted to eat part of the fellowship offering, which symbolized peace with God.

The question: What was the representation of the fat from the animal that was the Lord's?

Chapter 4
What I learned: The sin offering was for those who committed a sin out of weakness as opposed to outright rebellion against God.

The question: Is lust considered a sin caused by weakness?

Chapter 5
What I learned: The confession of sin shows a realization of sin, awareness of God's holiness, humility before God, and a willingness to turn from sin.

The question: What was the cost of the animals that were sacrificed?

Chapter 6

What I learned: The holy fire on the altar needed to continue to burn for the offerings because God started the fire, which represented his continual presence in the sacrificial system.

The question: Is this twenty percent penalty for stealing representative of "pain and suffering" in today's court system?

Chapter 7

What I learned: Blood represented the river of life and could not be used by people.

The question: Why was one of the offerings to God made with yeast?

Chapter 8

What I learned: Aaron's descendants were the only people to serve as priests. They stood in the gap between God and the people.

The question: What was the significance of putting blood on the lobe of Aaron's right ear, thumb of his right hand, and big toe of his right foot during ordination?

Chapter 9

What I learned: Fire came down from the presence of the Lord and consumed the burnt offering and the fat portions on the altar.

The question: Do Christians naturally have a problem believing the supernatural acts of God?

Chapter 10

What I learned: Aaron's sons, Nadab and Abihu, offered unauthorized fire and were consumed by fire from the Lord.

The question: Why didn't Nadab and Abihu take the commands of the Lord seriously?

Chapter 11

What I learned: So often we flirt with temptation, rationalizing that we at least kept the commandments and did not commit the sin.

The question: What was done to cleanse Israelites when they ate unclean food?

Chapter 12

What I learned: The bodily emissions and secretions made childbirth ceremonially unclean.

The question: Why were mothers required to bring a burnt and sin offering after childbirth?

Chapter 13

What I learned: Leprosy (defiling skin disease) represented diseases that were highly contagious and could be fatal.

The question: Why is a person defined as "clean" if the disease has spread over the entire body?

Chapter 14

What I learned: Many of God's laws may have seemed strange to the Israelites.

The question: Why did God decide to put a spreading mold in the house of the Lord?

Chapter 15

What I learned: The washing required when having a discharge or a monthly period was God-directed to maintain physical health.

The question: Why would a man with a discharge spit on someone who is clean?

Chapter 16

What I learned: The Day of Atonement was the greatest day of the year for the Israelites, where God covered their sins through their sacrifices.

The question: How often were the Israelites required to bring sin and burnt offerings during a given year?

Chapter 17

What I learned: Eating blood was a common practice in hoping to gain the characteristics of the slain animal.

The question: Why did God require death for those who sacrificed outside of the tabernacle?

Chapter 18

What I learned: Homosexuality is listed in this chapter as one of the unlawful sexual relations that destroys family life.

The question: Did God allow the Israelites to be forgiven for these sins, or were they killed?

Chapter 19

What I learned: God required the Israelites to leave the edges of the fields unharvested to provide food for travelers and the poor.

The question: Do the laws given in the Old Testament, such as refraining from tattoo marks, still apply today?

Chapter 20

What I learned: The detestable acts listed in this chapter were very common in the pagan nation of Canaan.

The question: Is there a difference between the statements "put to death" and "cut off from their people" (verses 4 and 5)?

Chapter 21

What I learned: The priests of the sons of Aaron were required to marry only virgins.

The question: What is the defect described by God that people may have had that didn't allow them to make sacrifices?

Chapter 22

What I learned: Animals with defects were not acceptable as sacrifices because they did not represent God's holy nature.

The question: Can we possibly meet the goal of giving our best time, talent, and treasure to God?

Chapter 23
What I learned: The Festival of Unleavened Bread reminded Israel of their escape from Egypt, and the Festival of Weeks praised God for a beautiful harvest.
The question: Why is the Day of Atonement the only festival that associates a punishment with not following it?

Chapter 24
What I learned: The punishment for blasphemy (cursing God) was being stoned to death.
The question: Why are punishments in the Old Testament so severe as compared to the New Testament?

Chapter 25
What I learned: At this time during the sabbath year (one year of seven to leave the fields unplowed for the poor), women were not paid to work.
The question: Why was the year of Jubilee not celebrated?

Chapter 26
What I learned: Calamity can happen not necessarily only from wrongdoing.
The question: Is there a way to know that tragedies we face are a result of sinful acts?

Chapter 27
What I learned: To prevent rash or unreasonable vows, Israelites who gave vows above the required offering had to pay twenty percent to be returned.
The question: Does God find any favor in redeeming vows?

BOOK FOUR

Numbers

Chapter 1

What I learned: Leviticus represents a book of laws, while Numbers is named for a numbering of the people in preparation for war.

The question: Is it a coincidence that Judah was the tribe that had the largest number of men (twenty years old) serving in the Army?

Chapter 2

What I learned: People were not known by a last name, but by their family, clan, and tribe.

The question: Was there any strategy or rationale known as to why the tribal camps were arranged in a specific order?

Chapter 3

What I learned: Levites had to be twenty-five years old before entering service and thirty years old before being admitted to full service.

The question: Were Levites given more responsibilities as they got older, or were responsibilities based on a set of skills?

Chapter 4

What I learned: The Lord put to death those who looked at the holy things.

The question: Were some Levite clans given more responsibilities than others due to the amount of Scripture devoted to the clans?

Chapter 5

What I learned: If a woman was guilty of cheating on her husband, the bitter water she was forced to drink caused her to miscarry.

The question: Did the feelings of jealousy have to be justified in any way before the wife was taken to the priest?

Chapter 6

What I learned: A Nazirite, possibly Samson, Samuel, and John the Baptist, was one who devoted time exclusively to serving God.

The question: Are there sins that we commit that are out of our control?

Chapter 7

What I learned: All the people participated in the maintenance of the tabernacle.

The question: Why does the Bible repeat the same verses instead of just using a summary at the end of the chapter?

Chapter 8

What I learned: The Levites themselves could be presented as a wave offering and could retire from regular service at age fifty.

The question: What does God mean when he says, "When I struck the firstborn in Egypt, I set them apart for myself"(verse 17)?

Chapter 9

What I learned: The Passover (second one) was an eight-day religious observance commemorating the Israelites' escape from slavery.

The question: Why were Israelites considered unclean when they were near a dead body?

Chapter 10

What I learned: The portable tabernacle signified God and the Israelites moving together.

The question: Why does Moses need to tell God to "rise up and return" (verses 35 and 36)?

Chapter 11

What I learned: When the Israelites complained about wanting meat (instead of manna), God provided it to them, but at a heavy cost.

The question: How does God differentiate between a complaint and a prayer?

Chapter 12

What I learned: Mariam (Moses's sister) and Aaron (Moses's brother) became jealous of Moses's authority, and God punished Mariam with leprosy for seven days.

The question: Why did Mariam receive a punishment, but there was no recorded punishment for Aaron?

Chapter 13

What I learned: One reason why the Israelites were afraid to enter the promised land was that the descendants of Anak ("owners") were seven to nine feet tall.

The question: Was it possible for the scouts to be somewhat fearful but still have faith in God's promises?

Chapter 14

What I learned: The Israelites failed to trust and obey God on ten separate occasions in the Old Testament.

The question: Does God punish us for being fearful, which represents a lack of faith?

Chapter 15

What I learned: The Israelites were given tassels on their garments as a reminder to remember the commands of the Lord.

The question: Why did God let other Israelites kill (stone) the Sabbath-breaker instead of God killing him?

Chapter 16

What I learned: Korah became jealous of Moses and wanted the power of being in the priesthood.

The question: Why did God end the lives of Korah, Dathan, and Abram by opening the earth and having them swallowed up?

Chapter 17

What I learned: God was angry about the complaining and grumbling; and consequently, he used Aaron's staff as a sign to the rebellious.

The question: Did the Israelites feel guilty when they felt that they were about to die?

Chapter 18

What I learned: Everybody was required to tithe to support the Lord's work.

The question: What was the punishment (if any) for the Israelites for not tithing?

Chapter 19

What I learned: When Israelites touched a dead body, they were unable to approach God in worship until they became ceremonially clean.

The question: What was the significance of purification on the third day when an Israelite was unclean for seven days?

Chapter 20

What I learned: Moses took credit for bringing water out of the rock, struck the rock twice instead of once, and did not enter the promised land.

The question: Would we ever be able to have a general understanding of the severity of God's punishments as it relates to our sin?

Chapter 21

What I learned: God used venomous snakes to punish Israel for complaining, and both the Israelites and Egyptians had a great fear of snakes.

The question: Why was it necessary for Moses to send spies (Jazer) instead of just getting a message from God?

Chapter 22

What I learned: A donkey asked Balaam why he beat him three times.

The question: Why did God tell Balaam not to go with Balak, then to go with instruction, and then stop his path with an angel?

Chapter 23

What I learned: Balak attempted to change the scenery and move from place to place to change Balaam's mind about cursing the Israelites.

The question: Why did Balaam continue to tell Balak to build seven altars and prepare seven bulls and seven rams after each change of location?

Chapter 24

What I learned: God spoke seven messages of the future and doom of Israel's neighbors through Balaam.

The question: Although Balaam was a sorcerer, did God bless him for loyalty to Israel?

Chapter 25

What I learned: Balaam involved the Israelites in a combination of sin and idolatry when he appeared to be on the Israelites' side previously.

The question: Why was God pleased with Phinehas for killing on behalf of God's truth?

Chapter 26

What I learned: After thirty-eight years, every Israelite over twenty years of age died except for Caleb, Joshua, and Moses.

The question: Did innocent Israelites die because of the corporate sinfulness of the Israelites?

Chapter 27

What I learned: The Lord told Moses that he was going to die in the desert and would be replaced by Joshua, son of Nun.

The question: Why were inheritances not given to the mother if a man died?

Chapter 28

What I learned: The Lord gave Moses instructions on daily offerings, monthly offerings, and Sabbath offerings.

The question: What was the significance of the amount of the offerings given to the Lord?

Chapter 29

What I learned: The Festival of Trumpets, the Day of Atonement, and the Festival of Tabernacles were holidays for the Israelites.

The question: Were the Israelites faithful in making their offerings during these holidays?

Chapter 30

What I learned: In ancient times, people did not sign written contracts, and a person's word was considered the binding contract.

The question: How did husbands and fathers judge whether a vow was a rash promise?

Chapter 31

What I learned: The Midianites were responsible for enticing the Israelites into Baal worship, and God had the Israelites kill every Midianite man.

The question: How did Moses feel when he was told that he was going to die after the war with the Midianites?

Chapter 32

What I learned: The Transjordan tribes, Reuben, Gad, and the half-tribe of Manasseh, originally did not want to cross the Jordan to the promised land.

The question: Why did Moses believe that the Transjordan tribes had selfish motives (not entering the promised land)?

Chapter 33

What I learned: The Israelites did not remove all the traces of pagan beliefs and practices, which led to the compromise of God's commands.

The question: Is it reasonable to have doubts if we truly do not understand all of God's purposes?

Chapter 34

What I learned: God created boundaries as an inheritance for each of the twelve tribes, and their inheritance was proportional to the size of the tribe.

The question: Are these places that were used to bound the land of Canaan still in existence today?

Chapter 35

What I learned: A person was sent to the city of refuge until the death of the high priest for an unintentional death, and put to death otherwise.

The question: Who were the avengers of blood in the Israelite families?

Chapter 36

What I learned: If a tribe received an inheritance, the inheritance would stay within that tribe because people must marry within that tribe.

The question: Does God make adjustments or exceptions to his laws, and under what circumstances?

BOOK FIVE

Deuteronomy

Chapter 1

What I learned: Because God had to condition the hearts of the Israelites, they spent forty years on a journey that should have lasted eleven days.

The question: Is being fearful a representation of a lack of trust and therefore qualified as sin?

Chapter 2

What I learned: The Lord informed Israel which parts of land to pass through and which to destroy through their journey in the promised land.

The question: Is there a list (or history) of these places traveled through by the Israelites in other books of the Bible?

Chapter 3

What I learned: After Moses pleaded with God about entering the promised land, God informed him to train Joshua because he would not enter.

The question: Did Moses blame the Israelites or himself for not being allowed to enter the promised land?

Chapter 4

What I learned: We will prosper for being obedient to God's laws, but this does not mean that we will not face trials.

The question: Does God consider the Ten Commandments more important than other laws he gave?

Chapter 5

What I learned: The Ten Commandments were being re-introduced, and we are morally guilty of violating these commandments.

The question: What is the meaning of the commandment, "You shall not misuse the name of the Lord your God" (verse 11)?

Chapter 6

What I learned: Moses commanded the Israelites to relate the Word of God to their daily lives and to not forget about God when they prospered.

The question: How does the promised land that the Israelites were traveling to compare to heaven?

Chapter 7

What I learned: God required Israel to completely destroy the enemy nations, leaving no survivors, including children.

The question: Are there occasions that we are punished by God for the sins of others?

Chapter 8

What I learned: The Israelites lost sight of the "quiet blessings" of God (not going hungry, feet not swelling in desert, clothing didn't wear out, and so on).

The question: How do our actions impact our blessings, or does God often just bless us through his grace?

Chapter 9

What I learned: Moses informed Israel that the Israelites were entering the promised land because of the wickedness of the enemy nations, not because of their righteousness.

The question: What role did the Amalekites and Moses play in the Israelites waiting forty years to enter the promised land?

Chapter 10

What I learned: Moses stated to the Israelites God's general expectations: respect, follow, love, serve, and obey.

The question: Are we truly in fear of God if we repeatedly do not follow his commands?

Chapter 11

What I learned: God expects us to obey his laws always, love him, and serve him with all our heart and soul.

The question: Is it possible for us to always follow God's laws?

Chapter 12

What I learned: God wanted the Israelites to completely get rid of pagan altars and idol worship in the land because the Israelites may be tempted.

The question: Is God's command of not eating blood related in any way to not eating the blood of animals?

Chapter 13

What I learned: God stated to the Israelites that if a loved one tempted them to seek other gods for worship, they should be the first to put the loved one to death.

The question: Why does God test us if he knows how we will react?

Chapter 14

What I learned: The purpose of the tithe is to fear the Lord and to put him first in our lives.

The question: Are there other laws equivalent to the laws of eating certain animals that no longer apply today?

Chapter 15

What I learned: God canceled the debts of the Israelites every seven years and reminded them that they were required to give to the poor.

The question: Other than money, how does God expect us to provide for the poor and needy?

Chapter 16

What I learned: God required all Israelites to bring a gift to the Festival of Tabernacles in proportion to the way God blessed them.

The question: What occurred during the Festival of Weeks and the Festival of Tabernacles? Do we have these festivals today?

Chapter 17

What I learned: When a person was put to death by stoning in order to purge evil, the person was taken outside the city gates and stoned to death.

The question: How did the witness of one being put to death feel about being the first to throw a stone that would kill?

Chapter 18

What I learned: Duties of ministers include teaching the people about God, setting an example of godly living, caring for the sanctuary and its workers, and distributing the offerings.

The question: What did the Israelites mean when they say, "Let us not hear the voice of the Lord our God nor see this great fire anymore, or we will die" (verse 16)?

Chapter 19

What I learned: In the Old Testament, the punishment fits the crime through the statement: "Show no pity, life for life, eye for eye, tooth for tooth, hand and foot for hand and foot. (verse 21)"

The question: Why do we no longer have cities of refuge for those who commit accidental crimes?

Chapter 20

What I learned: When the Israelites went to war against their enemies, God told the Israelites to offer peace as an alternative option.

The question: Why did God kill only the enemy men (as opposed to women and children) when all the enemy people were involved in idol worship?

Chapter 21

What I learned: A stubborn and rebellious son in Israel could have been stoned to death, but there was no evidence that such a law was carried out.

The question: What was the purpose of breaking the heifer's neck for atonement regarding unsolved murders?

Chapter 22

What I learned: If a woman who was not pledged to be married was raped, the rapist needed to pay a fine to the father and marry the woman.

The question: How did they go about proving virginity since it was the difference between life and death?

Chapter 23

What I learned: Outside of marriage, sex destroys relationships, and young people must be reminded about premarital sex.

The question: What was the assembly of Lord, and what was the reason behind the laws of not entering?

Chapter 24

What I learned: For newly married couples, Israelite men were free to stay at home and bring happiness to the married wife.

The question: Is it still true that each person dies for personal sin, or is it now possible to die resulting from other peoples' sins?

Chapter 25

What I learned: If a husband's brother did not marry the husband's wife when the husband died, the brother was spit on and insulted.

The question: What is the significance of the law that required a woman to have her hand cut off for grabbing a man's private parts?

Chapter 26

What I learned: The Israelites were required to give their tithe to the needy every third year.

The question: Does God have a preference on the type of the tithe we should give?

Chapter 27

What I learned: The Israelites could not use iron when building an altar for the Lord because this required cooperation from surrounding nations.

The question: Why is the word "secretly" in the verse, "Cursed is anyone who kills their neighbor secretly" (verse 24)?

Chapter 28

What I learned: The Lord states the blessings for obedience and curses for disobedience.

The question: Did it ever get bad enough to the point that the Israelites ate the flesh of their relatives due to their disobedience?

Chapter 29

What I learned: God does not reveal everything to us because our finite minds can't comprehend, we need to be more mature to understand, and we can't know what God knows.

The question: Why did Moses say that Israelites would never be forgiven if they choose to walk in their own way?

Chapter 30

What I learned: God gives us the option to be obedient and informs us that he will forgive us no matter how far we turn away.

The question: At any point in a person's life, can a person go without sin and always follow God's commands?

Chapter 31

What I learned: As the Israelites were a rebellious and stiff-necked people, we also continuously struggle with sin and need forgiveness.

The question: Were the Israelites not able to read at that time and consequently could only hear the laws?

Chapter 32

What I learned: Moses, as a song leader, reminded the Israelites of the mistakes made and that God's laws were life.

The question: How did Moses feel when God told him that he was going to die?

Chapter 33

What I learned: God blessed the tribes in different ways based on the talents within each tribe.

The question: Are God's blessings primarily based on our unique talents, on our decisions to follow God's requirement, or just by grace?

Chapter 34

What I learned: Moses climbed Mount Nebo to see the promised land and died there, although no one knows where his grave was located.

The question: How were the Israelites notified that Moses died?

BOOK SIX

Joshua

Chapter 1

What I learned: Joshua, Moses's aid for forty years, was told as the new leader of the Israelites to keep the book of the law on his lips and to study to be prosperous.

The question: Is it a sin to be afraid and not strong and courageous, as the Lord required of Joshua?

Chapter 2

What I learned: There have been several explanations as to why God may have justified Rahab's lie to protect the Israelite spies.

The question: Does God view sins equally, or does God view certain sins more harshly?

Chapter 3

What I learned: The Israelites did not drive out all of the Canaanites and ended up following their evil practices.

The question: Where do we now witness God's supernatural powers like when God parted the Jordan River for the Israelites?

Chapter 4

What I learned: God required Joshua to have a member of each tribe to obtain a stone to create a memorial to represent God's power for generations.

The question: What does it mean (in terms of our actions) to always fear God?

Chapter 5

What I learned: The Israelites were circumcised to represent cutting off the old life and beginning a new life because those previous Israelites had died.

The question: Are there still angels (of superior rank) currently as there were in the Old Testament?

Chapter 6

What I learned: Jericho was one of the oldest cities in the world, known for its military power and strength, and was destroyed by God.

The question: Did the Israelites have any doubt about God's complicated instructions for conquering the land?

Chapter 7

What I learned: Achan's sin of taking some of the plunder from Jericho caused his entire family to get stoned and caused the Israelites to lose the battle at Ai.

The question: Why does God punish the people for the sins of others?

Chapter 8

What I learned: The Lord allowed the Israelites to take the plunder from Ai (as opposed to Jericho) because the soldiers needed the food and equipment.

The question: Why did the Lord decide on a plan to sneak up on Ai as opposed to just destroying the city directly?

Chapter 9

What I learned: The Israelites were deceived by the Gideonites to make a treaty with them because they did not inquire of the Lord.

The question: Is it possible to inquire of the Lord about everything, or does the Lord expect us to use our gifts to make some decisions?

Chapter 10

What I learned: God had prolonged the days that the Israelites were at war by making the sun stand still and giving the Israelites victories.

The question: What is the meaning of the verse, "There has never been a day when the Lord listened to a human being" (verse 14)?

Chapter 11

What I learned: Despite the odds, Joshua followed every detail of God's commands and remained obedient.

The question: Were the other Israelites still somewhat fearful of the enemy nations although they did not follow Joshua and God?

Chapter 12

What I learned: This chapter lists all the kings defeated by Joshua on the east and west of the Jordan River.

The question: Why is it necessary for the defeated kings to be stated individually in the Bible?

Chapter 13

What I learned: The promised land was divided among the Israelites although some of the land was still conquered.

The question: Why was the tribe of Manasseh allowed to be divided into two tribes because of their own preferences?

Chapter 14

What I learned: Caleb received his inheritance of land promised to him forty-five years later for remaining faithful to God.

The question: Is there a reason that the Bible repeats that the Levites did not get an inheritance?

Chapter 15

What I learned: The boundaries of the towns of Judah regarding the promised land are included in this chapter.

The question: Can these towns and boundaries be clearly identified today?

Chapter 16

What I learned: The territory for Ephraim, Joseph's son and Jacob's grandson, was described, which included some Canaanites who were not dislodged.

The question: Why was a separate chapter written to describe only Ephraim's territory?

Chapter 17

What I learned: When Caleb received his land, he trusted God to drive out his enemies; but when Ephraim and Manasseh received theirs, they were afraid of the Canaanites.

The question: Is there a single map in existence that shows the territories listed in the Bible?

Chapter 18

What I learned: The Israelites were to divide the rest of the land into seven parts, and Joshua was to cast lots, although the method in which this was done was not stated.

The question: Why were the Israelites still afraid to completely wipe out the Canaanites, or did they now want to lose their labor force?

Chapter 19

What I learned: The Lord had the Israelites split up the conquered land instead of having one big undivided nation.

The question: Did the naming of all these territories have any significance? Were some territories more elegant than others?

Chapter 20

What I learned: The Levites were in charge of the cities or refuge, which had a purpose of preventing injustice, especially in cases of revenge.

The question: Why were the cities of refuge necessary, as opposed to requiring the Israelites to forgive their enemies and allowing God to avenge?

Chapter 21

What I learned: The Levites were to minister on behalf of all people, so they were given cities scattered throughout the land.

The question: Were the towns given to the Levites among the best of the Israelite towns?

Chapter 22

What I learned: The Reubenites, Gadites, and the half-tribe of Manasseh built an altar as a reminder that they all served the same God (not a pagan sacrifice).

The question: Are the different Israelite tribes like the different religions today that all serve the same God?

Chapter 23

What I learned: Joshua's farewell to Israel was to obey the Lord and not to intermarry with the pagan nations.

The question: How did Joshua mentally prepare himself for dying? What are God's expectations of us in terms of death preparations?

Chapter 24

What I learned: After (Joshua) laying down the fundamentals of having faith in God and removing idols, Joshua and Eleazer (a son of Aaron) died.

The question: How could a stone (verse 27) hear the words said by God as a witness for the Israelites?

BOOK SEVEN

Judges

Chapter 1
What I learned: The Israelites had difficulty removing the Canaanites because each city had to be conquered individually, and they were afraid.

The question: Was Caleb's younger brother permitted to marry Caleb's daughter because this type of marriage was acceptable?

Chapter 2
What I learned: Once Joshua died along with his generation, the new generation of Israelites served Baal and engaged in idol worship.

The question: Since the Israelites returned to their corrupt ways when the judges died, what accounted for the gaps in time between appointed judges?

Chapter 3
What I learned: Ehud, a left-handed man, was considered a judge with exceptional ability, and God made use of his unique talent in war.

The question: Did the judges work with the Levites to understand why the Israelites kept going back to do evil and worship Baal and Asherah?

Chapter 4
What I learned: One of the judges who led Israel was a prophetess named Deborah, whose main role was to encourage people to obey God.

The question: How was a leader of the enemy Canaanites, Sisera, able to escape on foot while all the other chariots were struck down?

Chapter 5

What I learned: Deborah sang a song with Barak that gave God credit for her victories but accused some Israelite tribes for not helping in battle.

The question: Who were princes of Israel, and what were their roles as Israelites?

Chapter 6

What I learned: The Israelites were so deep into Baal worship that they were willing to kill Gideon for destroying the Baal altar at night and building an altar for God.

The question: As Gideon did on two occasions, are we right to ask God for signs as opposed to just believing through prayer?

Chapter 7

What I learned: Through allowing some Israelites to not fight due to fear or how they drank water (like dogs), the Lord reduced the number of soldiers from thirty-two thousand to three hundred to give credit to God.

The question: Does God expect us to be fearful when the odds are against us, as he understands Gideon's fear of having enemy troops that outnumbered his troops?

Chapter 8

What I learned: Gideon had a son through a concubine named Abimelek who caused grief to his family and all of Israel.

The question: Why did Gideon ask his son to kill the kings? Were there reasons why the son (Jether) may have been afraid?

Chapter 9

What I learned: Abimelek killed sixty-nine of his seventy brothers (other than the youngest son) because he wanted to be in power as the first self-declared king of Israel.

The question: Do the connections between politics and religion in biblical times represent the relationship between politics and religion today?

Chapter 10

What I learned: The Israelites asked God for help as a last resort when they realized that the foreign gods could not help them.

The question: When the Israelites finally repented, who was the Israelite representative(s) who asked for help in being rescued?

Chapter 11

What I learned: Jephthah, an illegitimate son of Gilead, was used by God to lead Israel even though his own family rejected him.

The question: What rationale did Jephthah have to make a vow to sacrifice? What happened to Jephthah's daughter whom he vowed to sacrifice?

Chapter 12

What I learned: The tribe of Ephraim was angry and jealous that they were not invited to join in the fighting of the Ammonites. They went to war, and forty-two thousand Ephramites were killed.

The question: Did the Ephraimites consider the consequences of waging war with its own people?

Chapter 13

What I learned: When Manoah, Samson's father, asked the angel his name, the angel stated that his name was beyond understanding.

The question: Can we ever have a true understanding of angels and the actions they take in the Old Testament?

Chapter 14

What I learned: God used Samson to deliver the Israelites from the Philistines, but he wasted his God-given physical strength on ego and playing jokes.

The question: Did God already know that Samson was going to violate God's law by marrying a Philistine?

Chapter 15

What I learned: Samson took revenge for the Philistines killing his wife and father by killing one thousand Philistine men with a donkey's jawbone and burning their grain.

The question: Was Samson taking credit for his victory when stating, "I have killed 1000 men," or giving credit to God when stating, "You have given your servant this great victory" (verses 16 and 18)?

Chapter 16

What I learned: Samson allowed a prostitute, Delilah, to take advantage of him by continuous nagging, and she caused him to be blinded and imprisoned.

The question: Was Delilah ever punished for her deceit?

Chapter 17

What I learned: At this time, Israel had no king, and the Israelites did as they saw fit (committed idolatry).

The question: What inspired Micah to create his own idols? What motivated a young priest to conform to idol worship?

Chapter 18

What I learned: The priest who settled in Micah's house was disobedient due to carrying idols with him, claiming to speak for God, and performing signs at a house.

The question: Why did God allow the tribe of Dan to have the citizens of Laish killed if these citizens were at peace and secure?

Chapter 19

What I learned: Having concubines was an accepted part of Israelite society. Concubines only had some of the privileges of a wife. Concubines were used for sex, having children, and household help.

The question: What was the significance of the father of the concubine continuously asking the Levite to stay at his house?

Chapter 20

What I learned: A very bloody war took place between the tribes of Benjamin and the other tribes over the brutal killing of a concubine in the city of Benjamin.

The question: Was God punishing the Israelites by telling them to fight the Benjamites and allowing the smaller Benjamite tribe to defeat them?

Chapter 21

What I learned: Because the tribe of Jabesh Gilead did not care to assemble before the Lord, the Israelites killed every male and every female who was not a virgin.

The question: Which of the twelve tribes was linked to Jabesh Gilead? Why were they not present at the Lord's assembly?

BOOK EIGHT

Ruth

Chapter 1

What I learned: Instead of staying at Moab to start a new family, Ruth, through her faithfulness, went back to Israel to care for her widowed mother-in-law, Naomi.

The question: What is the difference between complaining to God and expressing pain (as Naomi did from losing her husband and two sons)?

Chapter 2

What I learned: Israelite law demanded that the corners of the field not be harvested so the poor and widows, such as Ruth, could have food.

The question: What was Ruth's task of gleaning? Did others besides the poor and widowed glean?

Chapter 3

What I learned: Naomi's advice was not seductive in telling Ruth to go find where Boaz was sleeping and lay below his feet.

The question: Why did Naomi tell Ruth to put on her perfume and her best clothes when going to the threshing floor?

Chapter 4

What I learned: Boaz presented his case to the "guardian-redeemer" (verse 3), which required him to marry Ruth, but he refused because he may have complicated his inheritance.

The question: Did Boaz have to buy Ruth as part of this witnessed transaction?

BOOK NINE

1 Samuel

Chapter 1

What I learned: Polygamy existed because it was an acceptable way of supporting women, and husbands could leave (divorce) wives who couldn't conceive.

The question: When Hannah dedicated Samuel to the Lord, does that mean that she was allowing Samuel to be used for ministry?

Chapter 2

What I learned: Eli was expected to put his two wicked sons to death because they treated God's offering with contempt by taking the offering of others for themselves.

The question: Did God punish Eli's two sons more harshly because they had a greater impact on God's people?

Chapter 3

What I learned: The Lord punished Eli because he was an excellent high priest but a poor parent through his lack of discipline of his sons.

The question: What does it mean when the Lord calls Samuel but "Samuel did not yet know the Lord"(verse 7), although he was a priest-in-training?

Chapter 4

What I learned: The Israelites believed that having the ark of the covenant with them would allow them to win the wars against the Philistines.

The question: Why was Eli sitting on the side of the road during a war?

Chapter 5

What I learned: The Philistines were governed by five rulers or lords: Gath, Ashdod, Ashkelon, Gaza, and one chief god, Dagon (although the Philistines had many gods).

The question: How were the Philistines able to continuously relocate the ark of God that was destroying its cities?

Chapter 6

What I learned: The Philistines devised a test to see if God caused their troubles. They had two cows go against their motherly instincts by sending the cows to Israel.

The question: Did the Israelites who were killed by looking inside the ark commit this sin intentionally or unintentionally?

Chapter 7

What I learned: Whatever holds first place in our lives or controls us is our god. (Samuel required the Israelites to rid themselves of all foreign gods.)

The question: Why did Samuel take a suckling lamb and sacrifice it as a whole burnt offering to the Lord when the Philistines came to attack the Israelites?

Chapter 8

What I learned: Because Samuel's sons were corrupt, the Israelites wanted a king because a king may be able to bring the tribes together, and they wanted to be like their enemies.

The question: Why did God honor their request for a king when God was unhappy with such a request?

Chapter 9

What I learned: Kish sent his son Saul to find his lost donkeys, which were all-purpose animals used for transportation, hauling, and farming.

The question: Did God choose an "inferior" king such as Saul because God was not in favor of having a "human" king over the Israelites?

Chapter 10

What I learned: Although Saul attempted to hide from being king of Israel, he was chosen by casting lots and using the Urim and Thummim to consult God.

The question: Why were Saul's looks and attractiveness discussed in Scripture?

Chapter 11

What I learned: Nahash the Ammonite threatened to gouge out the right eye of every Israelite to bring disgrace to Israel.

The question: Why did Saul need to threaten the Israelites to follow him by taking the pair of oxen, cutting them up, and sending them to messengers of Israel?

Chapter 12

What I learned: Samuel's words suggest that failing to pray for others is a sin.

The question: How did Samuel go about teaching the Israelites?

Chapter 13

What I learned: The Israelites had to rely on the enemy's (Philistines') blacksmiths to sharpen their swords, and the Philistines charged a very high price.

The question: Why did Saul take credit for Jonathan's defeat of the Philistines? Why did Saul become impatient when offering the burnt sacrifice?

Chapter 14

What I learned: Victory is neither guaranteed nor limited to the righteous, as Saul won a battle against the Philistines, although he was very foolish.

The question: Was Saul's son, Jonathan, wrong for not telling his father that he was going to fight against some of the Philistines even though God blessed him?

Chapter 15

What I learned: Saul disobeyed God by not completely destroying the Amalekites and keeping the plunder, which made God reject him.

The question: Why was Saul afraid of the Israelites by giving in to them and sinning against God?

Chapter 16

What I learned: The pouring of the anointing oil over David's head stood for holiness and was used to set people or objects apart for God's service.

The question: As what happened with Saul, how would we know that the Holy Spirit has left us and an evil spirit has entered instead?

Chapter 17

What I learned: David was criticized by his own brothers for trusting in God and fighting Goliath with a sling and stones and no coat of armor.

The question: Did the Israelites, other than David, lose trust in God by choosing not to fight Goliath for forty days?

Chapter 18

What I learned: Saul became jealous of David when he heard that "Saul has slain thousands and David his 'tens' of thousands"(verse 7).

The question: Was David's lack of action natural when Saul tried to kill him on two occasions?

Chapter 19

What I learned: Although Saul was attempting to kill David, a spirit came upon Saul, and he prophesied when finally catching up to David.

The question: During Saul's prophecy, why did Saul lay naked all day and all night?

Chapter 20

What I learned: Jonathan displayed an excellent example of true friendship through protecting David and not himself so that David could be the king of the Israelites.

The question: When Saul says to Jonathan, "You son of a perverse and rebellious woman" (verse 30), why did Saul speak of the woman when he was mad at Jonathan?

Chapter 21

What I learned: David protected himself while in the Philistine camp by acting unstable because the custom of the Philistines was not to hurt unstable people.

The question: What was the purpose of David going to Nob and visiting Ahimelek the priest?

Chapter 22

What I learned: Saul had eighty-five innocent priests killed because he thought that they were siding with David.

The question: Was there anything that these innocent priests could have done differently to prevent their deaths?

Chapter 23

What I learned: Saul wanted to kill David so badly that he thought that he received God's approval to kill him.

The question: Today, is there any object that represents the Urim and Thummim that the high priests (and David) used to make decisions?

Chapter 24

What I learned: David cut off a piece of Saul's robe to show Saul that he had been given the opportunity to kill him but did not due to respect for him.

The question: Why was David conscience-stricken for cutting off a corner of Saul's robe?

Chapter 25

What I learned: Samuel died, and David married Ahimoam of Jezreel and Abigail (wife of Nabal), whom the Lord killed for selfishness.

The question: Why was David so quick to go to war with Nabal for not letting his servants get food for David taking care of his flocks?

Chapter 26

What I learned: David again spared Saul's life by taking a jug and spear while Saul and Abner were sleeping.

The question: What was the reason why David had to show Saul again that he spared Saul's life after Saul kept making false promises?

Chapter 27

What I learned: David lied to one of the kings of the Philistines to have a place to live and avoid Saul.

The question: Since David was still running for Saul, does this imply that David did not believe Saul when Saul admitted to wrongdoing?

Chapter 28

What I learned: Saul consulted a spiritist (those who consulted the dead) because God did not answer him, and he was afraid of the Philistines.

The question: Was Samuel really raised from the dead? Did the spiritist really see Samuel when he told Saul his fate?

Chapter 29

What I learned: David, siding with the Philistine army through deception, was known by the Philistine commanders and knew that he may attack them.

The question: Did the Philistine, Achish, believe in God's power?

Chapter 30

What I learned: David used someone of relative insignificance to the Israelites, an Egyptian slave, to lead them to destroy the Amalekites.

The question: During the trip to attack the Amalekites, why did David not eat or drink for three days and three nights?

Chapter 31

What I learned: Saul killed himself because he did not want to be killed by the Philistines, and Saul's life ended with a lack of spiritual faith.

The question: Why did God allow the enemy Philistines to kill Jonathan, a man of great faith in God?

BOOK TEN

2 Samuel

Chapter 1

What I learned: David composed a lament for Saul, although he tried to kill David, and thanked Jonathan for their great friendship.

The question: Was it appropriate for David to kill the Amalekite messenger for lying, but for also bringing David the message that Saul and Jonathan were killed?

Chapter 2

What I learned: David ruled over Jordan for seven and a half years, but the rest of Israel did not accept his kingship at the time.

The question: Why was David willing to have this dagger match suggested by Abner (twelve of the best of both sides), which accomplished very little?

Chapter 3

What I learned: Although polygamy was socially acceptable for David at the time, God warned against it, and it became the root of many problems for David.

The question: In David's lament, when he states, "Should Abner have died as the lawless die," is he implying that the righteous did differently from the wicked?

Chapter 4

What I learned: Ish-Bosheth, son of Saul and weak-minded leader of Israel, was killed by two assassins, who were then killed by David.

The question: Why did many deaths take place by cutting off the heads of the enemy (beheading)?

Chapter 5

What I learned: David consulted God before attacking the Philistines and did not attack them face to face but through a water tunnel.

The question: Who was Hiram? What was his motivation to help David and build a palace for him?

Chapter 6

What I learned: David carelessly took the ark of God toward the City of David because he saw that any city that held the ark was blessed.

The question: Why did God consider the touching of the ark as capital punishment resulting in Uzzah's death?

Chapter 7

What I learned: God made certain that there was a prophet who was living during the reign of the kings of Israel so kings had an opportunity to listen and obey God.

The question: Did the prophet Nathan have any profound impact on David?

Chapter 8

What I learned: David conquered the surrounding nations and dedicated the plunder, silver, and gold of the nations to the Lord.

The question: Why did David kill his enemies so violently? Why did he allow portions of the enemy nations to live?

Chapter 9

What I learned: David wanted to show kindness to Saul's grandson and Jonathan's son, Mephibosheth, for political reasons and the promise he made to Jonathan.

The question: Why does the Bible emphasize the point that Mephibosheth was lame on both feet?

Chapter 10

What I learned: David attempted to make peace with the new king of the Ammonites, Hanun, but he listened to the bad advice of his commanders and went to war.

The question: If the Armenians and Ammonites ran away (fled) from Joab and his brother, Abishai, why did David still go to fight and kill their soldiers?

Chapter 11

What I learned: David lusted for Bathsheba instead of fleeing, and had her husband, Uriah the Hittite, killed because of David's sin.

The question: Do innocent people die as the direct result of sin? Was Uriah the Hittite truly innocent?

Chapter 12

What I learned: Through the prophet Nathan, God informed David through a story that he would be punished for killing his child.

The question: Why did David stop fasting when he realized that his child was dead?

Chapter 13

What I learned: David showed poor parenting skills by not punishing his son, Amnon, who raped his half sister, Tamar.

The question: Since David was unaware of his son Absalom's actions to kill his brother, Amnon, did David not have enough time to care for his family?

Chapter 14

What I learned: Absalom was very handsome, self-centered, and burned up Joab's barley fields for not listening to him.

The question: What was the significance of Joab sending the woman to King Talmai? What role does she have in the biblical context?

Chapter 15

What I learned: Absalom attempted to take the kingship from his father, David, by stealing the hearts of the Israelites through his kindness and good looks.

The question: Did David feel that his kingship was being taken away when he referred to his son as King Absalom?

Chapter 16

What I learned: When Absalom was given advice to sleep with his father's wives and concubines, the cultural significance was that he would be king.

The question: Why did David believe this time that the cursing of him by Shirei was from God and that Shirei did not kill him?

Chapter 17

What I learned: Hushai gave flattering advice to Absalom, which may have caused both Absalom and his advisor, Ahithophel, to die.

The question: Did God always recommend David to send spies to enemy territory, as opposed to God just giving information about it?

Chapter 18

What I learned: David went to war against the troops of his own son, Absalom, and David's commander, Joab, killed Absalom after his hair hung him alive.

The question: Did Joab's ego play a role in wanting to take credit to kill Absalom?

Chapter 19

What I learned: Joab never lost a battle as commander of David's army and was a brilliant and ruthless strategist, but never acknowledged God.

The question: What did Abishai, son of Zeruiah, mean when he said that Shimei the Benjamite "cursed the Lord's anointed" (verse 21)?

Chapter 20

What I learned: Perhaps due to jealousy, Joab killed Amasa, a possible replacement for Joab, and then went to attack Sheba, a troublemaking Benjamite.

The question: Who was the wise woman who saved a possible attack of a city by sending Joab the head of Sheba? What gave her such courage?

Chapter 21

What I learned: In many Near Eastern cultures, as with the Israelites, Saul's entire family was guilty of Saul's crimes and was punished by death.

The question: Did God validate this law that the family was a single unit and that all were affected by the sins of one family member?

Chapter 22

What I learned: During David's song of praise when he sings, "For I have kept the ways of the Lord" (verse 22), he was not denying that he has never sinned.

The question: Did David ever have any assistance in the writing of his songs of praise? How did he know what was important to say?

Chapter 23

What I learned: There were two elite groups who followed David who had to show unparalleled courage and great leadership: The thirty and the three.

The question: Did God play a role in choosing David's mighty men, or were they chosen by David or his priests?

Chapter 24

What I learned: Because David was too prideful, God gave David three choices of punishment (war, famine, or plague), and David chose the plague and seventy thousand died.

The question: Were all the Israelites who died guilty of pride as David was, or did God have another reason for killing these Israelites?

BOOK ELEVEN

1 Kings

Chapter 1

What I learned: While David was on his death bed, his son, Adonijah, attempted to set himself up as king, but then he sought God's forgiveness for his sins.

The question: What was the significance of the horns (corner posts) that both Adonijah and Joab clutched for God's forgiveness?

Chapter 2

What I learned: To establish his kingdom, Solomon ordered the executions of Joab, Adonijah (Solomon's brother), and Shimei (the person who cursed David).

The question: Did God find it necessary for Solomon to resort to killing to establish his kingdom?

Chapter 3

What I learned: Solomon asked for discernment and wisdom as opposed to long life, wealth, or death of his enemies, and God gave him discernment and wisdom, as he had asked.

The question: Are there specific requests that God expects us to ask for? Does God not recommend certain prayers?

Chapter 4

What I learned: Solomon was very organized in assigning officers of Israel through the wisdom given to him by God.

The question: Why did several of the officer names begin with the word "Ben," and what is the significance of this word?

Chapter 5

What I learned: Solomon was chosen by God to build the temple because he was a peacemaker and showed concern for the welfare of his workers.

The question: If Solomon was the wisest man in the world, why were there so many occasions when he didn't make use of his God-given wisdom?

Chapter 6

What I learned: God promises that his eternal presence would never leave the temple if the Israelites obeyed God's laws.

The question: Since God's dwelling place (the temple) had small inside dimensions, who was permitted to enter the temple, and why would that person enter the temple?

Chapter 7

What I learned: Solomon built himself a palace and hired Hiram, an expert craftsman, to assist him in building the temple's furnishings.

The question: Should churches use fine articles to enhance worship as Solomon and Hiram did with the temple?

Chapter 8

What I learned: Solomon asked for God's presence, for the desire to do God's will, for help with each day's needs, for a desire and ability to obey God's commands, and to spread God's kingdom to the world.

The question: Was the sacrificing of the sheep and cattle equivalent to tithing today?

Chapter 9

What I learned: Solomon used the non-Israelites who were supposed to be eliminated from Israel to do slave labor and commanded Israelite officials to supervise.

The question: Should Hiram have felt unpleased with the cities given to him by Solomon?

Chapter 10

What I learned: The Queen of Sheba used questions, riddles, and proverbs to test the wisdom of Solomon, but she was overwhelmed and began admiring him.

The question: Since living for God can be shown through blessings (Solomon's riches) or suffering, can we tell if someone is living for God?

Chapter 11

What I learned: Solomon turned away from God by marrying seven hundred wives, having three hundred concubines, and worshipping their gods.

The question: Did Solomon have all these wives and concubines due to lustful and sexual desires or to make potential alliances?

Chapter 12

What I learned: The Israelites became divided after the death of Solomon between two of Solomon's sons (Rehoboam—two tribes; and Jeroboam—ten tribes).

The question: What was done with the offering to the golden calves built by Jeroboam if the offerings were not intended for God?

Chapter 13

What I learned: A man of God informed Jereboam of his fate but was attacked by a lion after listening to another prophet instead of God.

The question: What was Jereboam's purpose of attempting to seize the man of God and making an offering at the altar?

Chapter 14

What I learned: Jereboam and Rehoboam both had sons named Abijah and one was sick and died (Jereboam's) while the other was a king.

The question: How old was Jereboam's son, Abijah, and what good did he do since God indicated that all Jereboam's family would be cut off?

Chapter 15

What I learned: Baasha, king of Israel, wiped out Jereboam's entire family because the worst sin was to cause all of Israel to sin.

The question: What is meant by the question, "Are they not written in the book of the annals of the Kings of Israel/Judah" (verse 23), and what are these annals?

Chapter 16

What I learned: Asa, king of Judah, was still king for thirty-eight years while many kings of Israel continued to commit evil in the eyes of the Lord.

The question: Since the Bible states that some kings of Israel did more evil than those who preceded them, does God view evil at different levels?

Chapter 17

What I learned: Elijah was a prophet sent by God to change hearts due to the kings of Israel who taught the Israelites to worship Baal.

The question: Why did the widow who God sent to met Elijah plan to die?

Chapter 18

What I learned: Elijah challenged the Israelites to choose between following him and God or to choose to follow the four hundred fifty prophets who worshiped Baal.

The question: Why did God allow Ahab an opportunity to turn back to God but not the four hundred fifty prophets who worshiped Baal?

Chapter 19

What I learned: Elijah prayed that he would die because he was very tired. The Israelites would not listen to him, and no other Israelites would support him.

The question: What is the significance of Elijah fasting exactly forty days and forty nights to travel?

Chapter 20

What I learned: Ahab refused to listen to God by not following him after helping Ahab win a battle on his behalf and sparing Ben-Hadad's life (his enemy).

The question: Did God kill Ahab primarily because he did not listen to God or because he led the Israelites away from God into idolatry?

Chapter 21

What I learned: Although Ahab was the most wicked king in Israelite history, God still forgave him when he repented for killing Naboth for not giving up his vineyard.

The question: Why did God allow Ahab to kill Naboth although Naboth was trying to uphold God's law by keeping the vineyard for his ancestors?

Chapter 22

What I learned: Both kings (Jehoshaphat, king of Judah; and Ahab, king of Israel) disregarded God's message of attacking by listen to the pagan prophets.

The question: What is the most efficient way to maximize our understanding of how God works to control evil?

BOOK TWELVE

2 Kings

Chapter 1
What I learned: The book of annals of the kings of Israel and the kings of Judah were history books and were written by writers directed by God for accuracy.

The question: Is there a significance as to how people die? Does it give ideas as to whether someone is going to heaven or hell?

Chapter 2
What I learned: Elijah was the second person mentioned in Scripture who left earth without dying, and Elisha asked to be his heir.

The question: Can our generation ever understand the mysterious events such as striking the water and splitting it or being consumed by fire?

Chapter 3
What I learned: Music accompanied the prophecy made by Elisha (through a harpist) that the kings of Israel, Judah, and Edom would defeat Moab.

The question: What was the purpose of the strong belief that the Baal worshipers had (and Moab) in child sacrifice?

Chapter 4
What I learned: The widow was told to continue bringing empty jars to her home to be filled with olive oil, which represented the amount of her faith.

The question: Why did the widow lie and say to Elisha's servant that everything was all right with her son when her son was dead?

Chapter 5

What I learned: Naaman was cured of leprosy by washing in a small, dirty river, which humiliated him due to his hero status.

The question: Did Naaman's faith solely depend on being cured of his leprosy?

Chapter 6

What I learned: The famine was so bad in Samaria, Israel's capital city, that mothers had to resort to eating their own children for Israel's disobedience.

The question: Why did the king of Israel refer to Elijah as "father" (verse 21)?

Chapter 7

What I learned: The king's officer lacked faith in God's deliverance and died after he saw the opening of the floodgates of heaven.

The question: Does God also put some people to death today for a lack of faith?

Chapter 8

What I learned: Elisha told Hazael that he was going to harm the Israelites because he was used as God's instrument for Israel's disobedience.

The question: Why did Ben-Hadad die after a thick cloth soaked in water was spread over the king's face?

Chapter 9

What I learned: God anointed Jehu as king of Israel to end Ahab's dynasty and to kill Joram (king of Israel), Azakiah (king of Judah), and Jezebel.

The question: Was the devouring of Jezebel's flesh representative of the external powers that are lost after death?

Chapter 10

What I learned: Jehu deceptively called an assembly of all Baal worshipers until it was completely filled, and then killed them all.

The question: What was the purpose of beheading the princes? Why was this so common?

Chapter 11

What I learned: Joash, Ahaziah's son who was hidden from Ahaziah's mother, Athaliah, from being killed, was made king at seven years old.

The question: Why did Athaliah want to kill her entire royal family line when Jehu killed her son?

Chapter 12

What I learned: Although Joash did what was right in the eyes of the Lord originally, he eventually turned to idols, his kingdom went out of control, and he was assassinated.

The question: Why does the Bible state that he did what was right in the eyes of the Lord, but does not state his worshiping of idols?

Chapter 13

What I learned: Even though Elisha was dead, God still performed miracles through him when a dead man was brought to life when touching Elisha.

The question: When Elisha told Jehoash to strike the ground representing defeat of Aram, how would he have known how many times to strike?

Chapter 14

What I learned: Amaziah became arrogant when defeating the Edomites by picking a fight with Jehoash, king of Israel, and was soundly defeated.

The question: Why did God allow the kings of Israel and Judah to go to war with each other? Did God favor one of the two?

Chapter 15

What I learned: Azariah, also known as Uzziah, reigned fifty-two years as king of Judah and did what was right, but did not remove the idols in the high places.

The question: Why is so little mentioned in the Bible about Azariah's devotion to God during his long reign? Why did the Lord afflict him with leprosy?

Chapter 16

What I learned: Ahaz ordered Uriah the priest to build a new pagan altar seen in Damascus and required him to give offerings although God didn't approve of the altar.

The question: Since Ahaz followed the practices of the Canaanites by sacrificing his son, and follow the practices of God by sacrificing offerings at the altar, did he support God, Baal, or both?

Chapter 17

What I learned: Because of the many public and private sins of their Israelites and their worshiping of other Gods, God completely destroyed Israel.

The question: Can we obtain some understanding of why God was so patient and merciful to both ourselves and the Israelites?

Chapter 18

What I learned: The kings of Judah paid the kings of Assyria to prevent them from attacking them.

The question: Was Hezekiah telling the king of Assyria the truth when he states, "I have done wrong" (verse 14)?

Chapter 19

What I learned: When the powerful king of Assyria threatened Hezekiah, Hezekiah prayed to the Lord, and the Lord acknowledged his prayer.

The question: Can angels put people to death as was done with 185,000 people in the Assyrian camp?

Chapter 20

What I learned: Although God told Hezekiah, who was very ill, that he was going to die, God added fifteen years to Hezekiah's life after he prayed to God.

The question: Why did God specifically add fifteen years to Hezekiah's life and chose to punish Israel after Hezekiah's death for his mistake?

Chapter 21

What I learned: Manasseh and his son, Amon, (kings of Judah after Hezekiah died) did evil in the eyes of the Lord by involving Israel in occult practices.

The question: Did these evil kings believe in God, or did they believe in God and just choose not to follow God's laws?

Chapter 22

What I learned: Josiah was one of the few kings who obeyed God completely and was rewarded by not seeing God's disaster of Israel while he lived.

The question: Why do we not value the truths in the Bible as Josiah did with the book of the law?

Chapter 23

What I learned: Josiah was remembered as Judah's most obedient king through recognizing sin, eliminating sinful practices, and attacking the cause of sin.

The question: Could Josiah have done anything different in raising his two sons who both did evil in the eyes of the Lord?

Chapter 24

What I learned: The sins of Manasseh were so evil that God was not willing to forgive Judah and allowed Babylon to overthrow Judah.

The question: What are possible reasons why God may decide not to forgive some sins?

Chapter 25

What I learned: The king of Babylon completely destroyed Judah to the point where there was no food to eat and no way to run from the Babylonian army.

The question: What happened to Zedekiah, king of Judah, when he was captured and sent to Babylon? When did Jehoiachin become king of Judah?

BOOK THIRTEEN

1 Chronicles

Chapter 1

What I learned: Genealogies show that God does not just care about nations, but special people and individuals to build God's kingdom.

The question: How did God decide what individuals should be included in these genealogies since the genealogies do not give an exhaustive list?

Chapter 2

What I learned: The author gives some insight on some people in the Bible in this lengthy genealogy.

The question: Why did the author decide to add insight for some people but not others?

Chapter 3

What I learned: This chapter gives the genealogy of David's sons, the king of Judah (beginning with Solomon's son) and the royal line after the exile.

The question: What is meant by an exile? What is the significance of the royal line?

Chapter 4

What I learned: Jabez is remembered for his prayer request, which is, "Oh, that you would bless me and enlarge my territory and keep me from harm so that I will be free from pain" (verse 10).

The question: Due to a lack of faith, is it expected that people can be completely free of pain during their time on earth?

Chapter 5

What I learned: Even though the armies of Reuben, Gad, and Manasseh had instinct and skill as soldiers, they continued depend on God for victory.

The question: Is the descendant of Joel, Baal, son of Reaiah, connected in any way to Baal, the god worshipped by the Canaanites?

Chapter 6

What I learned: Many temple musicians were mentioned in the genealogies, which emphasizes the importance of lesser known people who serve God.

The question: Why are so few women included in the genealogies?

Chapter 7

What I learned: When the number of clans was stated in this chapter, the number only refers to "fighting men" (verse 2).

The question: What is the meaning of "fighting men" stated in this genealogy? What determines a "fighting man"?

Chapter 8

What I learned: Shaharaim divorced both of his wives and married other wives, which was not God's will but was permitted.

The question: What was the significance of the names of sons such as Esh-Baal and Merib-Baal?

Chapter 9

What I learned: This chapter includes the genealogy of the Levites, who were responsible for taking care of the house of the Lord.

The question: To what extent do we speak out about the sins of others, or does God want us to focus more on our own sins (captivity due to sins of others)?

Chapter 10

What I learned: Saul was both actively and passively disobedient to God by actively consulting a witch and passively not asking for God's forgiveness.

The question: Related to God's refusal to answer Saul's prayer, under what conditions may the Lord choose not to answer our prayers?

Chapter 11

What I learned: David had three mighty warriors who sacrificed their lives to get water for David, and he gave the water to God as an offering.

The question: Although the Moabites were enemies of the Israelites, why was the Moabite Ithmah considered one of the thirty mighty warriors?

Chapter 12

What I learned: David surrounded himself with great warriors who were mentally tough and determined to serve God and David.

The question: What does it mean when we experience the Holy Spirit to accomplish God's purposes, as what took place with David's warriors?

Chapter 13

What I learned: David was angry with the Lord because the Lord's wrath broke out against Uzzah for Uzzah's death resulting from touching the ark.

The question: Can Christians have any understanding of God's methods of blessings and punishments?

Chapter 14

What I learned: Before David made a major decision requiring an attack of the Philistines, he inquired of God asking for his presence and guidance.

The question: Because David had so many sons, why is so little mentioned in the Bible about the women who raised his sons while David was in battle?

Chapter 15

What I learned: God's wisdom is complete and his judgment infallible although we may not understand the reasons for God's judgments in this life.

The question: Why did David blame the Levites for incorrectly returning the ark to Jerusalem when it may have been him who did not know God's instructions?

Chapter 16

What I learned: Four elements are found in David's songs: remembering what God has done; telling others about God; showing God's glory; and offering gifts of self, time, and resources.

The question: How did David bless his family, as stated in the last verse in this chapter (verse 43)?

Chapter 17

What I learned: God's promise to David had two parts: David's descendants had to follow God's laws (conditional) and a son of David would occupy the throne (Jesus).

The question: Why did God not want a warrior, such as David, to build his temple?

Chapter 18

What I learned: When God gave victory to David over his enemies, he dedicated the articles collected from his enemies to God and not himself.

The question: What happened to the articles dedicated to the Lord? Who benefited from this dedication?

Chapter 19

What I learned: Due to Hanun misreading David's intentions of showing kindness, Hanun embarrassed David's envoys by shaving their beards and cutting their garments.

The question: Was David responsible for too much bloodshed (killed forty-seven thousand total charioteers and foot soldiers) as opposed to verbal negotiation?

Chapter 20

What I learned: Kings went out to battle during the spring harvest because farmwork eased off and the armies could live off the land.

The question: Was it literal or figurative that the man who killed Jonathan, son of Saul, had six fingers and six toes?

Chapter 21

What I learned: When we become tempted (as David was to take a census), we must examine our inner desires to understand why the external temptation is so appealing.

The question: Does the Bible give us understanding of protecting individual Christians through prayer and why these individuals suffer due to the sins of others?

Chapter 22

What I learned: David gave Solomon instructions for building the temple and taught him about being strong and courageous and following God's laws.

The question: Can Christians have any understanding of God's methods of blessings and punishments?

Chapter 23

What I learned: David made preparations for building the temple through taking a census of the Levites and assigning responsibilities to them.

The question: What is significant about the age of twenty, which was required to do Levitical duties?

Chapter 24

What I learned: The genealogy of the division of the priests (twenty-four groups) is listed here (each group served for two weeks in the temple).

The question: Were the temple duties automatically assigned to people or could other Israelites volunteer to serve?

Chapter 25

What I learned: Musicians were divided into twenty-four groups to match the twenty-four groups of Levites, and each group worked a term, then rotated.

The question: If David set apart an Israelite to play music using the harps, lyres, and cymbals, were the sons of that Israelite also playing music?

Chapter 26

What I learned: When Israelites won wars, some of the plunder was used to make repairs to the temple.

The question: What are some of the differences between what we are obligated to give and the extra that we can give (duty versus joy and love)?

Chapter 27

What I learned: David did not take count of the number of men twenty years old or younger because the Lord had promised to make Israel numerous.

The question: Are certain numbers (twenty-four thousand) in the Bible to serve as approximations or actual values?

Chapter 28

What I learned: The Lord searches every heart, so it makes no sense to hide any thoughts or actions since he knows our worst and loves us anyways.

The question: What was so important about weighing the gold and silver for the articles of the temple?

Chapter 29

What I learned: Six principles David gave to Solomon were: (1) get to know God personally, (2) learn God's commands, (3) worship God with wholehearted devotion, (4) serve God, (5) be faithful, and (6) don't be discouraged.

The question: What are the primary reasons why Christians do not follow these principles?

BOOK FOURTEEN

2 Chronicles

Chapter 1

What I learned: Solomon asked for wisdom (the ability to make good decisions) and knowledge (the practical know-how necessary to handle common matters).

The question: Does God prefer us to ask for wisdom and knowledge instead of wealth, longer life, and the consequences of our enemies?

Chapter 2

What I learned: Because the Israelites were knowledgeable about agriculture but knew little about metalworking, Solomon hired foreigners to assist with the temple.

The question: Although Hiram (assisted Solomon with trade) was a ruler of a nation with many gods, did Hiram believe in God since he helped Solomon?

Chapter 3

What I learned: The cubit (unit of measurement for designing the temple) was approximately 20.5 inches.

The question: Is it challenging to convince Christians to invest so much money in beautifying the church as Solomon did with the temple?

Chapter 4

What I learned: God gave very specific instructions regarding the expensive temple furnishings, which were carefully followed by Solomon.

The question: How did the huge crowds respond to the beauty of the temple? Did it meet their expectations?

Chapter 5

What I learned: The temple represented God's covenant with Israel and God's laws (the tablets of the Ten Commandments were kept in the temple).

The question: What is meant by the statement, "The glory of the Lord filled the temple of God" (verse 14)?

Chapter 6

What I learned: Solomon, through his prayer of dedication, reminds God of his promises and states to God how he should act.

The question: Does God need to be reminded of his promises when God knows all?

Chapter 7

What I learned: God gave four conditions for forgiveness: humble ourselves by admitting our sins, pray to God, seek God continually, and turn from sinful behavior.

The question: What type of symbols of God's presence do we have today that are equivalent to fire coming from heaven (to consume the burnt offerings)?

Chapter 8

What I learned: Although Solomon carefully followed God's instructions in building the temple and making sacrifices, he married many pagan women, which led to his downfall.

The question: How did Solomon use his wisdom and riches to address his sin of lust and marrying pagan women who worshiped other gods?

Chapter 9

What I learned: King Solomon was greater in riches and wisdom than all the other kings of the earth, and other kings gave many gifts just to hear him.

The question: Did God support Solomon in how he used his riches? How concerned is God regarding how we make use of wealth?

Chapter 10

What I learned: The Israelites split into two when Solomon died; ten of the tribes followed Jeroboam and were called Israel, and Judah and Benjamin called their nation Judah.

The question: Why did God want to split the Israelites into two kingdoms?

Chapter 11

What I learned: The Levites continued their strong belief in God and left Jeroboam because they were worshiping idols, and they strengthened the southern kingdom ruled by Rehoboam.

The question: Does God still want Christians to have large families such as Rehoboam's family (twenty-eight sons and sixty daughters) to build the kingdom?

Chapter 12

What I learned: At Rehoboam's peak of popularity and power, he and the Israelites abandoned the Lord but were forgiven after confessing their sin.

The question: Who is Iddo the seer who deals with genealogies?

Chapter 13

What I learned: True faith in God ran stronger and deeper in Judah than in Israel, but it was still not up to God's standards.

The question: Are we as Christians living up to God's standards? What are those standards since we are expected to sin?

Chapter 14

What I learned: Asa, king of Judah, was given peace because he did what was good and right in the eyes of the Lord.

The question: Why did so many armies want to go to war against Judah?

Chapter 15

What I learned: Azariah told Asa not to give up because his work would be rewarded not just on earth but in the life to come.

The question: When Asa stated that all who do not seek God should be put to death, what was the evidence of not seeking the Lord?

Chapter 16

What I learned: Instead of asking God for help as he did previously and receiving peace, Asa sought help from the pagan king, Ben-Haded, and sinned.

The question: What is the balance between seeking responsible medical help through the help of doctors and prayer through the help of God?

Chapter 17

What I learned: Jehoshaphat, Asa's son, initiated a nationwide religious education program because the people of Judah were biblically illiterate.

The question: Other than the discussion of God's laws, what other topics were likely discussed in these programs?

Chapter 18

What I learned: Ahab, king of Israel, chose to listen to his hired false prophets regarding going to war because they only told him what he wanted to hear.

The question: As with the prophet Michiah, who was punished for telling the truth, what messages does God want to send to us when we are punished for disobedience?

Chapter 19

What I learned: Jehoshaphat told leaders to (1) realize they are judging for God and (2) be impartial and honest, be faithful, and act only out of fear of God.

The question: Was there a difference between the wrath of the Lord concerning Jehoshaphat and the wrath of Jehoshaphat's appointed leaders?

Chapter 20

What I learned: Jehoshaphat made an alliance with the king of Israel, Ahaziah, who was wicked, and God destroyed the alliance by wrecking ships used for trade.

The question: How do we know when to fast, as Jehoshaphat decided to have the people of Judah fast?

Chapter 21

What I learned: Jehoram was a very evil king who killed all his brothers, and God gave him an incurable disease that made his bowels come out. He then died, to no one's regret.

The question: Did Jehoram's marriage to Athaliah (daughter of Jezebel, the most wicked queen Israel has ever known) contribute to the level of evil of Jehoram?

Chapter 22

What I learned: Since no one in the house of Ahaziah, Jehoram's son, was powerful enough to retain the kingdom, his evil mother, Athaliah, ruled the land.

The question: Did the officials of Judah truly believe that Ahaziah sought the Lord with all his heart when the Bible says that he did evil in the eyes of the Lord?

Chapter 23

What I learned: Jehoiada the priest showed his strength by taking the place of the king from the evil queen mother, Athaliah, who was executed like Jezebel.

The question: Why did Jehoiada, who knew that Baal worship led by Queen Athaliah was wrong, take seven years to show his strength?

Chapter 24

What I learned: Joash originally did what was right in the eyes of the Lord, but when the priest Jehoiada died, Joash abandoned the Lord and killed Jehoiada's son.

The question: Why was Jehoiada, who was not a king, buried with the kings in the city of David, but Joash, who was a king was buried elsewhere?

Chapter 25

What I learned: Amaziah, king of Judah, paid Jehoash, king of Israel, a hundred talents for one hundred thousand fighting men, but God disapproved and Amaziah sent back the troops.

The question: If Amaziah did not follow God wholeheartedly, why is it stated that he did what was right in the eyes of the Lord?

Chapter 26

What I learned: After many accomplishments, Uzziah got prideful and burned incense, which was the role of the Levites, and God punished him with leprosy.

The question: Does God still give success to those who do not seek the Lord (Uzziah was given success only when he sought the Lord)?

Chapter 27

What I learned: Jotham was generally a good king and lived for God, but his people remained corrupt and did not listen to him.

The question: What is meant when the Bible states, "He did not enter the temple of the Lord" (verse 2) as his father had done?

Chapter 28

What I learned: Ahaz offered sacrifices to the gods of Damascus because he believed that if they helped Damascus, they could help him also.

The question: Since the Israelites knew that their sin/guilt was already great, although God allowed Israel to defeat Judah, did the Israelites take any other action for God?

Chapter 29

What I learned: King Hezekiah did what was right in the eyes of the Lord and fixed the damage done by his father by having the temple repurified.

The question: Were the Israelites in any way influenced by the impact Hezekiah had on Judah?

Chapter 30

What I learned: Although Israel had strayed away from God, Hezekiah, king of Judah, sent a letter to them to celebrate the Passover, but some mocked him.

The question: What was meant in the Old Testament by "being purified" (verse 18) to properly partake in the Passover? Are there similarities to this today?

Chapter 31

What I learned: We may not worship idols made of wood and stone, but wealth, pleasure, prestige, and material possessions can also serve as idols.

The question: Are there still Christians that rely on the tithes of others to live and minister to God?

Chapter 32

What I learned: When the king of Assyria threatened Hezekiah, he did everything he could to deal with the situation, then trusted God for good results.

The question: As Hezekiah did not do successfully, how do we differentiate between pride and self-confidence?

Chapter 33

What I learned: Hezekiah's son, Manasseh, did much evil in the sight of the Lord, but when he prayed, the Lord forgave him and told Judah to serve the Lord.

The question: Do we need to be punished to gain a deeper respect for God and his great power?

Chapter 34

What I learned: In Josiah's day, boys were considered men at age twelve and understood the responsibilities as king by age sixteen.

The question: What does God mean when he tells Josiah that he would be buried in peace and would not see the disaster coming to Israel?

Chapter 35

What I learned: Not realizing that God was working through a pagan king, Josiah did not listen to Pharaoh Necho and was killed.

The question: Did Josiah make a mistake by not consulting God regarding the message given by a pagan king?

Chapter 36

What I learned: God gave Jerusalem to King Nebuchadnezzar, king of Babylon, because the people of Israel and Judah kept turning away from him.

The question: Why did King Nebuchadnezzar ask Zedekiah, king of Judah, to take an oath in God's name? Why did Zedekiah refuse?

BOOK FIFTEEN

Ezra

Chapter 1
What I learned: God used a pagan, the king of Persia, to conquer the land, but allowed Judah and Israel to rebuild and return from exile.

The question: Are the other Israelites who needed additional incentives to return to Jerusalem like Christians who need incentives to attend church?

Chapter 2
What I learned: This chapter lists the exiles who returned from Babylon to Jerusalem while also giving offering for rebuilding the temple.

The question: How should the amount that we give to God compare to the standard ten percent of income?

Chapter 3
What I learned: Some of the people wept because the new temple built under Zerubbabel would not be as glorious and elaborate as the previous temple built by Solomon.

The question: Did the people have a strong understanding of why they were giving so many different offerings? Did they all give for the same reasons?

Chapter 4
What I learned: While David was on his deathbed, his son, Adonijah, attempted to set himself up as king, but then he sought God's forgiveness for his sins.

The question: When opposition came from Judah's enemies to rebuild the temple, fear and doubt overcame Zerubbabel, and the building of the temple was halted.

Chapter 5

What I learned: The non-Jews who were nearby attempted to hinder the task of rebuilding the temple by trying to obtain authorization to build the temple.

The question: How do we best judge when to speak up for our faith to those who clearly don't believe?

Chapter 6

What I learned: Although the kings of Assyria killed many Israelites during the time of Israel's disobedience, God changed the king's attitude to help rebuild the temple.

The question: If God has the power to change the attitude of people to do his will, why doesn't he do this more often?

Chapter 7

What I learned: Ezra was a teacher of the law, started a religious education program, and regularly studied the law and served God faithfully.

The question: Did King Artaxeres, a pagan king, have the support of God to punish by death anyone who did not obey God's law?

Chapter 8

What I learned: Ezra, before making his nine-hundred-mile journey to Jerusalem on foot, recruited Levites and prayed for a safe journey instead of using soldiers.

The question: What are the differences between the more serious prayer given by Ezra and superficial prayers that maybe given by Christians?

Chapter 9

What I learned: Ezra prayed to God on behalf of the people of Israel for marrying the neighboring people who had detestable practices (intermarriage).

The question: How does God decide when he should grant mercy and when he should offer punishment?

Chapter 10

What I learned: Although God forgave our sins as believers of Christ, we are still required to confess our sins by recommitting ourselves to God and asking for forgiveness.

The question: Did God hold the leaders (Levites) to a higher standard to follow God's rules? Does God deliver different punishments based on our relationship with God?

BOOK SIXTEEN

Nehemiah

Chapter 1

What I learned: Nehemiah demonstrated the elements of effective prayer: (1) praise, (2) thanksgiving, (3) repentance, (4) specific requests, and (5) commitment.

The question: What was Nehemiah's brother's, Hanani, role in the rebuilding of the wall? Did he assist in helping Nehemiah?

Chapter 2

What I learned: Nehemiah's approach to rebuilding the wall was to get firsthand information, consider the situation, then present a realistic strategy, which was good problem-solving technique.

The question: What lesson was Nehemiah giving us when God brought about Sanballat the Horonite and Tobiah the Ammonite to stop the rebuilding process?

Chapter 3

What I learned: There was one group, the nobles of Tekoa, which was the only group, who was lazy and did not support the building project.

The question: Is it unusual for women to help in the actual repair of the wall or a church?

Chapter 4

What I learned: Nehemiah demonstrated two parts of real service to God: talking with him (prayer) and walking with him (acting on behalf of God).

The question: Why did God support the rebuilding of the wall under the leadership of Nehemiah if God doesn't actually need a wall to protect Israel?

Chapter 5

What I learned: Nehemiah told the richer Jews that it was wrong for them to charge poorer Jews excessive interest and to force children into slavery.

The question: What were some of the reasons why certain Israelites were poor and some were rich?

Chapter 6

What I learned: Although Tobiah and Sanballat tried to intimidate Nehemiah and some of the nobles tried to attack Nehemiah personally, he completed the wall.

The question: How do we know as Christians when to pray to get out of situations or pray to get through situations?

Chapter 7

What I learned: Nehemiah put his brother, Hanini, and Hananiah, the commander of the citadel, in charge because they were men of integrity and feared God.

The question: How accurate are the genealogical records in the Bible? Do they always include all descendants?

Chapter 8

What I learned: Nehemiah was the governor of the land and political leader, and Ezra was the priest/scribe and spiritual leader. Both divided the leadership.

The question: Does God expect us to perform actions to remind us how far God has brought us, as when the Israelites built temporary shelters?

Chapter 9

What I learned: The Israelites confessed their sins and thought back to the many times they were forgiven.

The question: Like the Israelites did, why do we repeatedly fail God when we are aware of the consequences of our sins and know God's laws?

Chapter 10

What I learned: The Israelites made a commitment to the tithe (ten percent), which was to be used to support the priests and the Levites.

The question: Although the Bible emphasizes the tithe from the Israelites, did God expect greater contributions?

Chapter 11

What I learned: Nehemiah asked the Israelites to move inside the city walls, but since only a few volunteered due to inconvenience, Nehemiah casted lots.

The question: When the Bible discusses casting lots, what factored into the process? How was it done?

Chapter 12

What I learned: This chapter emphasizes the importance of music used for temple worship instituted by David.

The question: Was it difficult for the Israelites to know people of their past since last names were not used and several Israelites had the same names?

Chapter 13

What I learned: A tendency to sin, as the Israelites had, must be dealt with swiftly, otherwise, it may overpower us.

The question: What were some of the root causes of why the Israelites chose to sin? Why do we choose to sin intentionally?

BOOK SEVENTEEN

Esther

Chapter 1

What I learned: When Queen Vashti chose not to parade before King Xerxes in an all-male party, he made a law never to see her again.

The question: Although Persia was a world power and King Xerxes was the wealthiest person in the world at the time, did he thank God for his great wealth?

Chapter 2

What I learned: Esther, who was told by Mordecai not to reveal her identity to King Xerxes, allows us to see that it is best to remain quiet until the time is right.

The question: How are the characteristics of Queen Esther, "lovely figure, beautiful, attractive," viewed in the Bible compared to today?

Chapter 3

What I learned: Haman wanted to destroy all the Jews and have them bow down to him as a god, but Mordecai stood up for God and did not bow down.

The question: Why was the city of Susa bewildered when the edict was issued to kill all the Jews?

Chapter 4

What I learned: Esther risked her life to save Mordecai and the Jews by approaching the king and asking for mercy because of the edict to destroy all Jews.

The question: Is it considered selfish when we as Christians don't stand up for what is right in hostile situations?

Chapter 5

What I learned: Esther carefully planned her meeting with King Xerxes and was very courageous by risking her life and security for the Jews.

The question: Are the purchasing of guns against the idea that God is to serve as our ultimate security?

Chapter 6

What I learned: Mordecai saved King Xerxes from being assassinated and was not rewarded, but God waited until the right time to reward Mordecai.

The question: Why didn't Haman ask the king who was being honored before offering an opinion about how Mordecai should be honored?

Chapter 7

What I learned: Haman was impaled on the same pole that he built to impale Mordecai because of Haman's hatred of the Jews.

The question: What was the primary reason why Haman specifically hated the Jews? How should Christians feel about those of different religions?

Chapter 8

What I learned: Mordecai and Esther were now being rewarded by God for being faithful and risking their lives for the Jews.

The question: How can Christians strengthen their faith like Mordecai and Esther so that we would be willing to risk our lives for God?

Chapter 9

What I learned: Mordecai sent letters to all the Jews to have them celebrate Purim, which was a reminder that God gave the Jews relief from their enemies.

The question: Are terrorist organizations such as ISIS enemies of God and Christians, and will God give us relief from them?

Chapter 10

What I learned: Moredcai was held in high esteem by the Jews and was second in power to King Xerxes.

The question: Although it is clear that God is in control, does our faith waiver because we don't understand what happens to us?

BOOK EIGHTEEN

Job

Chapter 1

What I learned: Satan, originally an angel of God, had to get permission to strike everything that Job had, but could not put a hand on Job.

The question: Does God use Satan to make us suffer in an attempt to strengthen our faith, or do we have some control of our suffering?

Chapter 2

What I learned: Satan obtained approval from God to afflict Job with painful sores to test Job's faith.

The question: Is God's use of Satan to test Job specific to Job because God knew the strength of his faith?

Chapter 3

What I learned: Job spoke out about his suffering and wished that he had never been born.

The question: Will God choose to reveal to us why we suffer, or does God find it best that we don't understand?

Chapter 4

What I learned: Eliphaz insisted that Job was suffering as a result of his sin because people who do right by God should not suffer.

The question: How difficult is it to not fear and trust God when we are left with so many unanswered questions?

Chapter 5

What I learned: Eliphaz gave good general advice about God's discipline when we do wrong, but the advice didn't apply in Job's case.

The question: Is it truly possible to understand the pain we endure?

Chapter 6

What I learned: Job was under so much grief and pain that he was willing to die and rid himself of his pain.

The question: Does God take a position in the Bible on suicide?

Chapter 7

What I learned: Job talked directly to God about his feelings and wanted God to leave him alone because he was enduring so much pain.

The question: How does God expect us to react when we suffer? How does God expect us to talk to him?

Chapter 8

What I learned: Bildad also believed that God does not punish just people, but is correct in saying that God must be our ultimate source of security.

The question: Is it not true that all Christians are unjust and can be subject to any form of punishment as God sees fit?

Chapter 9

What I learned: Job made the claim that God would make his wounds multiply for no reason.

The question: When we suffer, is it expected for us to ask for immediate healing, or can God view our prayers as being impatient?

Chapter 10

What I learned: Job felt that through so much affliction, God wanted to destroy him. He felt sorry for himself.

The question: Does God sometimes reveal to us through others why we suffer as individuals, or does God always hold back information?

Chapter 11

What I learned: Of Job's three friends that offered advice to him about his current situation, Zophar was the most arrogant and insensitive.

The question: Since all have sinned, is it possible that Job should confess to other sins, and if so, what sins had Job committed?

Chapter 12

What I learned: Job reminds us that God's wisdom far exceeds the knowledge given by any people here on Earth.

The question: What does Job mean when he says he is "blameless" (verse 4)? Can any Christians on earth make such a claim?

Chapter 13

What I learned: Job told God to stop frightening him with terrors and asked how many wrongs and sins he had committed.

The question: Are we ever in a position to tell God (as Job did) what he should do differently when his ways are always right?

Chapter 14

What I learned: Job discussed that through sickness, loneliness, and disappointment, life was not fair.

The question: Although suffering can strengthen our faith and improve our dependence on God, would Christians ever encourage suffering?

Chapter 15

What I learned: Eliphaz continued to argue with Job in the second round of discussions and states, "What do you know that we do not know" (verse 9)?

The question: Is Eliphaz's statement accurate when he states that God places no trust in his holy ones?

Chapter 16

What I learned: Job was afraid that God abandoned him, although he appealed directly to God and to God's knowledge of his innocence.

The question: If Job's friends are miserable comforters, why does he continue to listen to them?

Chapter 17

What I learned: We must not evaluate life only in terms of this present world, as Job's friends never once mentioned life after death.

The question: What does Job mean when he states, "Who else will put up security for me" (verse 3)? What security should we look for on earth?

Chapter 18

What I learned: Bildad rejected Job's speech because it did not fit with his outlook on life.

The question: Is Bildad's characterization of a sinner accurate for a Christian or one who does not believe in God?

Chapter 19

What I learned: Even through all the pain and losses Job endured, Job reminded faithful and confident that justice would triumph through God.

The question: Can we determine whether our suffering is a test from God or a result of our sinfulness?

Chapter 20

What I learned: Punishment for evil people may not be given here on earth but on the final judgment.

The question: What are some differences between the Christian and the evil person since both are sinners?

Chapter 21

What I learned: When the wicked prosper despite their sin, Christians may question why they should try to do good.

The question: How much understanding should we have of the afterlife? What are the roles of church leaders to strengthen our understanding?

Chapter 22

What I learned: Eliphaz continued to tell Job to repent of his sins and submit to God although he had done this already.

The question: Can any person be blameless before God's eyes at any point in life?

Chapter 23

What I learned: Job feared God because he could not see God, because God can do whatever he pleases, and because he had no explanation for his suffering.

The question: Does God punish us for unintentional sin? Do we have commonly have hidden sin unaccounted for?

Chapter 24

What I learned: The arguments presented in this chapter of rewarding the wicked and punishing the righteous do not sound like Job.

The question: What is God's plan for the murderer who kills the innocent, poor, and needy in the night?

Chapter 25

What I learned: Bildad expressed to Job how little human power is in comparison to God's power.

The question: What does Bildad mean when says that the stars are not pure in God's eyes?

Chapter 26

What I learned: Job sarcastically attacked Bildad because he wanted to analyze and give advice instead of loving and showing compassion.

The question: How does Job understand the concept of power as it relates to humans if God is all-powerful?

Chapter 27

What I learned: Although Job stated that the Lord had made his life bitter, he would not say anything wicked.

The question: Did Job have a right to say to God, "I will never admit you are in the right until I die"(verse 5)?

Chapter 28

What I learned: No leader of group of leaders can produce enough knowledge or insight to explain the totality of human experience, only God can.

The question: What impact do Christian books have on obtaining wisdom?

Chapter 29

What I learned: Job walked a fine line between bragging about past accomplishments and recalling good deeds.

The question: Did Job feel the need to inform God of his past accomplishments because he believed his friends in that God was punishing him for sin?

Chapter 30

What I learned: Job stated that he cried out to God, but God didn't answer.

The question: When we pray to God to stop or ease our suffering, does our faith play a role in God's response or lack of response?

Chapter 31

What I learned: Job presented many inward and outward sins that he himself had not done and presented this to God.

The question: Because lust was the first sin mentioned by Job, is this one of the most common sins by Christians?

Chapter 32

What I learned: A younger bystander, Elihu presented the idea that Job wasn't suffering because of sin—he was sinning because he was suffering.

The question: Does it become difficult to trust and have faith in God when our suffering cannot be truly understood?

Chapter 33

What I learned: Our greatest test may be that we must trust God's goodness even though we don't understand why our lives are going in a certain way.

The question: Did Elihu believe that he understood more about God than Job?

Chapter 34

What I learned: Although we do not want to suffer, suffering can be both helpful and harmful.

The question: Is Elihu correct when he says, "God brings on them what their conduct deserves" (verse 11)?

Chapter 35

What I learned: Elihu stated that God does not always answer because of the arrogance of the wicked or empty pleas.

The question: What are the differences between prayers that God will answer later and that God will never answer?

Chapter 36

What I learned: God is incomprehensible, and we can obtain some knowledge about him and still have more questions than answers.

The question: What answers can the Bible provide for us about the severity of our suffering and how to minimize our suffering?

Chapter 37

What I learned: Elihu used illustrations of clouds, rain, and thunder to show God's power.

The question: Are we ever in a position to tell God to do things when God is all-knowing?

Chapter 38

What I learned: God spoke to Job and questioned him on natural occurrences such as rain, light, hail, snow, and lightning.

The question: Was God making the point that if a person doesn't have the answers to acts of nature, then the person will not have answers to suffering?

Chapter 39

What I learned: God asked Job several questions about the behavior of animals to help Job recognize his power.

The question: What answers do nonbelievers give to God's questions about the animal kingdom?

Chapter 40

What I learned: When Job was given the opportunity to plead his case as requested in previous chapters, Job remained silent.

The question: Is it always better to pray our way through the suffering as opposed to asking for knowledge as to why the suffering is occurring?

Chapter 41

What I learned: God told Job that he could not stand up to God if he could not even stand up to a Leviathan (considered to be a crocodile).

The question: Did the Leviathan really exist in biblical times? What was God's role for it?

Chapter 42

What I learned: After Job repented for questioning God's sovereignty and justice, God restored Job and gave him greater blessings than he had before.

The question: Does God give us some blessings to allow us to see reasons to trust him and have faith in those situations we don't understand?

BOOK NINETEEN

Psalms

Chapter 1
What I learned: Knowing and meditating on God's Word are the first steps toward applying it to our everyday life.

The question: What are reasons why Christians don't meditate on God's Word consistently?

Chapter 2
What I learned: If people do not serve God, they will serve someone, something, or their own selfish desires.

The question: What does it mean in our actions if we fully submit to Christ?

Chapter 3
What I learned: We can overcome fear by trusting God for his protection in our darkest hour.

The question: Should trusting God be a difficult task based on circumstances?

Chapter 4
What I learned: We must search our hearts for hidden sins and trust God will forgive us and listen to us when we continue to fall short.

The question: When David says, "Tremble and do not sin when you are on your beds" (verse 4), can there be a point in our lives when we do not sin?

Chapter 5
What I learned: As we grow closer to God, our sensitivity to sin increases, and we cannot excuse even the smallest of sins.

The question: Are atheists considered enemies of God?

Chapter 6

What I learned: On many occasions, we want God to show mercy for us but give justice to others.

The question: Is it fair to expect justice for our enemies but not ourselves?

Chapter 7

What I learned: Instead of taking matters into his own hands, David cried out to God for justice against his enemies because it is God who avenges.

The question: When God allows the violence of the wicked to kill innocent people, are these people really innocent?

Chapter 8

What I learned: God has given us great authority, but this comes with great responsibility.

The question: How is praise different between growing up as children and as adults?

Chapter 9

What I learned: When asking God to help us, we must always consider our motives.

The question: In our current time, who can be considered our enemies and the wicked people whom we want God to judge?

Chapter 10

What I learned: The wicked appear to succeed with no regard of God's law.

The question: Why does God allow those who believe in him to suffer, but those who don't believe in him to kill Christians?

Chapter 11

What I learned: As David did, we must use our tests and challenges as opportunities to grow because being a good Christian doesn't make us immune to them.

The question: When acts of nature occur that kill righteous people, how do we convince others that God is in control?

Chapter 12

What I learned: David asked for help because he believed no one was faithful and people used flattery, deception, and boasting.

The question: What does David mean when he says, "The Lord will keep the needy safe and protect us from the wicked" (verse 7)?

Chapter 13

What I learned: David claimed that God was not acting fast enough to David's distress.

The question: Do we have an impact on God's timing of relieving us from pain and distress?

Chapter 14

What I learned: We become atheists in practice when we rely more on ourselves than on God.

The question: How does God look on the atheist who does good deeds for God's people, such as giving to the poor?

Chapter 15

What I learned: The depth of our eternal relationship with God can often be measured by the way we reflect his standards in our daily activities.

The question: Why did David give guidelines to living a blameless life when none of us are blameless?

Chapter 16

What I learned: Many people fear death because they can neither control nor understand it.

The question: Do people feel abandoned by God because of a lack of safety and civil rights since actions don't take place in enough time to keep people safe?

Chapter 17

What I learned: We must not conclude that we have somehow missed God's protection when we experience troubles.

The question: Is it appropriate for David to ask God to have his enemies die by the sword for his protection?

Chapter 18

What I learned: God doesn't promise to eliminate challenges, but instead promises to give us strength to meet challenges so we can grow.

The question: Are cherubim ("angels") still used to protect us as in David's time?

Chapter 19

What I learned: David asked if a person could discern that person's own errors and asked God to forgive his hidden faults.

The question: Is it a sin if we do not talk to others about God?

Chapter 20

What I learned: David knew not to trust in the power of humans, but only in the power of the Lord.

The question: Does God answer our prayers, or does he listen to our prayers?

Chapter 21

What I learned: We may lose a great deal—families, jobs, material possessions—but we cannot be shaken from God's favor.

The question: Should we praise God more for the gifts he gives to us or the sicknesses and tragedies that he does not bestow upon us?

Chapter 22

What I learned: David accurately gave a depiction of the suffering the Messiah would endure hundreds of years later, which had some similarities to his own suffering.

The question: When David said that he was forced to trust God, is this fully accurate if God gives us choices to trust him or not?

Chapter 23

What I learned: Death casts a frightening shadow over us because we are entirely helpless in its presence, and strength and courage cannot overcome it.

The question: Do some Christians believe that death is determined by whether we take the right paths, or is death predetermined regardless of our actions?

Chapter 24

What I learned: God cannot hear us or speak to us if we build a wall of self-deception.

The question: Do Christians truly have an adequate understanding of who God is?

Chapter 25

What I learned: Our first step to receive guidance is to read the Bible, where we will perceive God's direction in our lives.

The question: Do we need more guidance and protection from human enemies or enemies of temptation, such as lust or money?

Chapter 26

What I learned: "Blameless" does not mean the same as "sinless." David just wanted his name cleared of false charges.

The question: Should Christians focus more on helping nonbelievers or other Christians?

Chapter 27

What I learned: We can conquer fear by trusting in the Lord, who brings salvation.

The question: Do we find ourselves reminding God of previous prayers or needs when our prayers don't appear to be answered?

Chapter 28

What I learned: David asked God to hear his cry for mercy and not turn a deaf ear to him.

The question: What are reasons why God may remain silent when we call on him?

Chapter 29

What I learned: God reveals his power through mighty miracles such as breaking giant trees with his voice alone.

The question: What are miracles that God does currently that humans cannot explain?

Chapter 30

What I learned: If we depend on God for our security, we won't be shaken when worldly possessions disappear.

The question: Are there actions we take that anger God but are not sins?

Chapter 31

What I learned: Stephen showed absolute dependence on God even when being stoned to death because he was simply passing from God's earthly throne to eternal care.

The question: Many Christians say that they have faith in God, but do we trust him in all circumstances?

Chapter 32

What I learned: We must recognize our sinfulness, realize that our sin is against God, admit our sins, trust God's willingness to forgive, and accept his forgiveness.

The question: When David says, "Blessed is the one whose sin does not count against them," does this mean intentional sin may not be considered?

Chapter 33

What I learned: Thousands of Christians have been beaten to death, whipped, fed to lions, or executed.

The question: Does God choose not to save some Christians from death for reasons only known to God?

Chapter 34

What I learned: God may allow Christians to go without to help grow more dependent on him.

The question: Is it more accurate to say that God delivers us "from" our troubles or that God delivers us "through" trouble?

Chapter 35

What I learned: God hears every prayer, but answers according to his wisdom.

The question: Is it natural for us to tell God to answer us during times of suffering and persecution?

Chapter 36

What I learned: Because the wicked have no fear, nothing stops them from sinning, and they move forward as if nothing will happen to them.

The question: Are those who have no fear of God considered to be "wicked" (verse 1), as David describes?

Chapter 37

What I learned: Worrying reveals a lack of faith that God loves us and is in control.

The question: Are there some poor people who cannot get out of their current situation so that God can see who helps the poor and needy?

Chapter 38

What I learned: David admitted that he deserved to be punished, but asked God not to punish him while he was angry and to forgive him for his sins.

The question: Are there levels of sins that God gives different degrees of punishment for? How does God handle repeated sins?

Chapter 39

What I learned: When we have complaints about our situation, we should discuss them directly to God and not with others.

The question: Are there specific tasks that God requires us to do in this life to prepare for eternity?

Chapter 40

What I learned: David states in verse 11, "Do not withhold your mercy from me, Lord, may your love and faithfulness always protect me."

The question: Why do Christians not tell others about God in the workplace?

Chapter 41

What I learned: Even when our closest friends and relatives forsake us, God is always on our side.

The question: When David asked God to allow him to rise up and repay his enemies, did he intend to repay in a positive or negative manner?

Chapter 42

What I learned: The writer of this psalm was thirsty for God through continuously seeking him and trying to get a deep understanding of God.

The question: What are the different ways that we can deepen our relationship with God?

Chapter 43

What I learned: The sons of Korah questioned why God has rejected them. Why God is disturbed with them?

The question: Does God actually reject us as the sons of Korah indicated?

Chapter 44

What I learned: Our suffering may not be a punishment but a battle scar that demonstrates our loyalty.

The question: What are all the different reasons on why God makes us suffer?

Chapter 45

What I learned: A messianic psalm prophetically describes the Messiah's future relationship to the church, his body of believers.

The question: What does the author mean by "virgin companions" (verse 14)?

Chapter 46

What I learned: It seems impossible to consider the end of the world without being consumed by fear, but God is our refuge even in the face of total destruction.

The question: Does God expect us to be naturally fearful in the times of trouble although we know God's mighty power?

Chapter 47

What I learned: We can't describe God completely, but we can tell others what he has done for us.

The question: Does God still subdue nations today as he did in early biblical times?

Chapter 48

What I learned: We must continue to praise God for protection from our enemies and our own bad decisions.

The question: What role does Mount Zion (Jerusalem) play in our current time as Christians?

Chapter 49

What I learned: To have treasure in heaven, we must place our faith in God, pledge ourselves to obey him, and utilize our resources for God.

The question: What does God expect for us to accomplish on earth before we die?

Chapter 50

What I learned: God judges people who treat him lightly for silence or superficially religious people who just follow rituals.

The question: Aren't we treating God lightly when we sin intentionally?

Chapter 51

What I learned: Because we are born as sinners, our natural inclination is to please ourselves rather than God, so we must keep asking for mercy and forgiveness.

The question: Are we truly sorry for certain sins that we continue to commit?

Chapter 52

What I learned: We must measure all we do by the rule of God's Word, not how effective we do a sinful task.

The question: Do we engage in subtle deceitfulness and boast about it primarily because of wealth?

Chapter 53

What I learned: The reason why people reject God and believe he doesn't exist has much to do with people's sinfulness.

The question: How much effort should be exerted in convincing the "fool" (atheist) that God does exist?

Chapter 54

What I learned: David asked God to repay evil to his enemies, which represented confidence in God's promise.

The question: What are other reasons why we sacrifice freewill offerings to God?

Chapter 55

What I learned: Daniel and Peter followed the pattern of praying morning, evening, and noon to maintain correct priorities throughout the day.

The question: When David's enemies were attacking him, wouldn't it be natural for him to be overwhelmed with fear and pray to God?

Chapter 56

What I learned: On many occasions, we waiver between faith and fear, but we must trust God in the midst of our enemies.

The question: In the present day, who can be considered as our enemies?

Chapter 57

What I learned: When confronted with verbal attacks, the best defense is to simply be quiet and praise God whom we have confidence in.

The question: How do we decide when verbal attacks should be confronted or ignored?

Chapter 58

What I learned: David's forceful sense of justice turned back on him when he occupied the throne.

The question: Should we talk to God about how to punish our enemies as David did, or should we just allow God to avenge us?

Chapter 59

What I learned: David had learned to turn negative consequences into reminders of God's faithful presence.

The question: When it appears that evil people are rewarded for doing evil things, why do we engage in these evil practices when we know they are wrong?

Chapter 60

What I learned: David asked for aid against the enemy because God rejected Israel, and he found human help to be useless.

The question: When acts of nature end up being catastrophic, can Christians have an understanding of God's control over such events?

Chapter 61

What I learned: David stated that his heart grew faint as he called on God in an unknown place.

The question: Do our prayers have different levels of power, and does God hear them differently?

Chapter 62

What I learned: God weighs us on trusting him and working for him and not on honor, wealth, and prestige.

The question: Should more time be invested in spreading the message of the power of God or working on our own personal shortcomings?

Chapter 63

What I learned: If we are lonely or thirsty for something lasting in our lives, we must remember that God alone can satisfy our deepest longings.

The question: Other than sin, what may be the cause of a weak relationship with God?

Chapter 64

What I learned: Satan can tempt us in our weakest areas when we least expect it.

The question: For Christians, what are our weak areas where we falter the most and Satan is most successful?

Chapter 65

What I learned: Although we may feel overwhelmed by the multitude of sins we may commit, God will forgive if we ask sincerely.

The question: How often do we need to give praise to all that God has done for us? In what matter should this be done?

Chapter 66

What I learned: Our confession of sin must be continual because we continue to do wrong.

The question: If we intend on doing right, what makes us sin so often?

Chapter 67

What I learned: This psalm speaks of the fulfillment of the Great Commission when Jesus commanded that the gospel be taken to all nations.

The question: Why don't all Christians spread the gospel to others?

Chapter 68

What I learned: David praised God for his protection and provision, and we must continue to trust God because his promises, in time, will be fulfilled.

The question: What does it mean that salvation is freedom from sin and death?

Chapter 69

What I learned: When we are completely beaten down, we must continue to pray no matter how bad things become because God hears our prayers.

The question: Do different Christians go through different trials because God equips us with some characteristics, but not others?

Chapter 70

What I learned: As many of our prayers are filled with requests for ourselves and others, we must remember to praise God for all he has done for us.

The question: Isn't it natural for us to state (as David did) not to delay help although God helps using his own timing?

Chapter 71

What I learned: Although there are many physical limitations when we get old, older Christians must continue to serve God and tell others about him.

The question: What did the psalmist mean when he says, "Though I know not how to relate to all God's saving acts" (verse 15)?

Chapter 72

What I learned: God emphasizes the importance of helping the needy and afflicted, which means that Christians should have a plan to help the poor.

The question: Should we ask God to oppress and destroy our enemies as David and Solomon did, or should we ask God to forgive our enemies?

Chapter 73

What I learned: Though our courage and strength may fail, we know that we will be raised to serve God forever.

The question: Why does our flesh fail us so often? Does our world care of such failures?

Chapter 74

What I learned: If we persist in intentionally sinning against God, his patience with us may run out.

The question: How can we better understand God's timing when allowing those who hate God to prosper?

Chapter 75

What I learned: As limited human beings, we can't understand God's perspective about time and must trust God's timing.

The question: When we pray, should we offer suggestions about his timing or ask God to adjust his timing as it relates to life events?

Chapter 76

What I learned: The psalm writer, Asaph, informs us that we should make vows to the Lord and fulfill them.

The question: Are we hesitant to make vows to strengthen God's kingdom due to time, lack of faith to see results, or risk of failure to fulfill the vow?

Chapter 77

What I learned: When we are in distress, we must cry out to God and remind ourselves of God's mighty deeds and miracles.

The question: If Christians know that God is all-knowing, then why do many people in the Bible believe that God forgets about them when we are in trouble?

Chapter 78

What I learned: The next generation must be made aware of the mistakes committed against God through some sort of religious education.

The question: Are there differences between rebelling against God as the Israelites did and any other biblical sin?

Chapter 79

What I learned: Wrath and judgment often fell on entire nations because of the sins of people within those nations.

The question: Does God give us guidelines on how we must handle suffering due to actions we did not cause?

Chapter 80

What I learned: Before restoration must come repentance, which means we must humble ourselves, turn to God, and acknowledge our sins.

The question: Is it expected that we will continuously sin, which is why we must continue to ask God for forgiveness after we repent?

Chapter 81

What I learned: We should conduct an inventory of our spiritual life and determine what impact God has on our daily decisions.

The question: What are some of the commands that God gives us that Christians do not listen to well?

Chapter 82

What I learned: Believers are commanded to pray for authority members that we may live peaceful and quiet lives in all goodness and holiness.

The question: Does God hold preachers, judges, and leaders to different levels of punishment for sin if their sins affect many others?

Chapter 83

What I learned: Sometimes we must be humbled by adversity before we look up and see the Lord.

The question: When we seek the Lord for prayer, should we invest more time in asking for protection from our enemies or the strength to endure pain?

Chapter 84

What I learned: Going into a church building can help us step aside from the busyness of life so that we can quietly meditate and pray.

The question: Why do the psalmists often ask God to "hear my prayers" (verse 8) when they know that God hears our prayers?

Chapter 85

What I learned: The more we seek God's righteousness and his kingdom, the more we will see everything taken care of by God.

The question: What does it mean to fear God? Do intentional sins represent a lack of fear in God?

Chapter 86

What I learned: No matter how well we know and follow God, we can always ask him to increase our awareness of him and improve our obedience.

The question: Will a closer relationship with God generally result in God answering more prayers?

Chapter 87

What I learned: God gives everyone the opportunity to enter into the community of believers and be registered in the Book of Life.

The question: Are we enemies of God if we don't believe in God's existence?

Chapter 88

What I learned: This is one of the few psalms that gives no answer of expression of hope.

The question: Does God give us some control on minimizing our suffering? How do we know if our suffering is due to our actions?

Chapter 89

What I learned: Righteousness, justice, love, and faithfulness are central characteristics of the way God rules.

The question: Did the Christians of the past need to see God's miracles to have increased faith in God?

Chapter 90

What I learned: Realizing that life is short helps us use the little time we have more wisely and for eternal good.

The question: Does God expect us to do certain things before we die? How do these actions prepare us for the next life?

Chapter 91

What I learned: By entrusting ourselves to his protection and pledging our daily devotion to him, we will be kept safe.

The question: What role do we have in protecting ourselves from harm?

Chapter 92

What I learned: We can never say "thank you" enough to parents, friends, leaders, and especially God.

The question: How should our activities change when serving the kingdom of God as we get older?

Chapter 93

What I learned: "Your statutes, Lord, stand firm: holiness adorns your house for endless days" (verse 5).

The question: What actions by Christians most negatively affect our morality in an attempt to be more like Christ?

Chapter 94

What I learned: The Bible says that no discipline seems pleasant at the time, but only temporary pain and future righteousness.

The question: Can we separate the differences between God's discipline on us and God choosing not to act according to his timing?

Chapter 95

What I learned: We are kept from God's blessings through an ungrateful heart, not submitting to God, hardening our hearts, and stubbornly testing God.

The question: Do we all lose faith in God at some point in our lives?

Chapter 96

What I learned: We can sing about God, tell others about God, worship God, give God glory, bring offerings to God, and live holy lives.

The question: Why do we choose not to talk about God in certain public places?

Chapter 97

What I learned: We must assess whether our lifestyle, work, play, buying habits, and giving hurt or help the less fortunate.

The question: When the Bible states that God guards the lives of his faithful ones, is this a general statement due to the crimes of the wicked?

Chapter 98

What I learned: God is merciful when he punishes, and he overlooks no sins when he loves.

The question: Do non-Christians recognize God's righteousness to the nations? What do they expect to see in order to believe in God?

Chapter 99

What I learned: How easy it is to treat God lightly in everyday life.

The question: What understanding should Christians have about cherubim and other angels?

Chapter 100

What I learned: To acknowledge God, we must appreciate God as Creator, accept his authority in every detail, agree with his guidance, and express our thanks for his love.

The question: What does the psalmist mean when he says, "Enter his gates with thanksgiving and his courts with praise" (verse 4)?

Chapter 101

What I learned: Because our friends and associates can have a profound influence on us, our friends and associates must be godly, truthful, and faithful to God's Word.

The question: What does David mean when he says that he wants to live a "blameless" (verse 2) life?

Chapter 102

What I learned: The psalmist asked God to hear his prayer, to not hide his face, and to answer quickly.

The question: What does the psalmist mean when he states, "Because of your great wrath, for you have taken me up and thrown me aside" (verse 10)?

Chapter 103

What I learned: God does not treat us as our sins deserve or repay us according to our iniquities.

The question: Although God forgives us of our sins if we ask him, does God still punish the sin based on repetition and who was affected?

Chapter 104

What I learned: The earth is built on God's foundation, and it can never be moved by anyone other than God.

The question: How do other religions believe the earth is created?

Chapter 105

What I learned: If God seems far away, we should persist in our search for him because God rewards those who sincerely look for him.

The question: Did God give harsher punishments to the Egyptians because of the harshness toward the Israelites?

Chapter 106

What I learned: We have seen God's great miracles, but sometimes find ourselves enticed by the world's gods—power, convenience, fame, sex, and pleasure.

The question: Do Christians and non-Christians view God's miracles differently? What is defined as a miracle?

Chapter 107

What I learned: Those who have never truly suffered may not appreciate God as much as those who have matured under hardship.

The question: Do we all eventually represent one of the four types of people: wanderers, prisoners, sick, and storm-tossed?

Chapter 108

What I learned: "Give us aid against the enemy, for human help is worthless" (verse 12).

The question: What are some of the differences in prayers for survival and prayers for victory?

Chapter 109

What I learned: An imprecatory psalm is a call for God to judge the wicked.

The question: When our enemies persecute us, should we ask God to judge our enemies or ask God to forgive them?

Chapter 110

What I learned: Many people have a vague belief in God, although they refuse to accept Jesus as anything more than a great teacher.

The question: Are Christians expected to understand everything in the Bible regarding what is stated about differences between God and Jesus?

Chapter 111

What I learned: The only way to become truly wise is to fear (revere) God.

The question: What actions are shown by Christians that demonstrate a fear of God?

Chapter 112

What I learned: When we trust God completely to take care of us, we will find that our other fears, even death itself, will subside.

The question: Is it possible to live in this life with no fear of the actions of others or its circumstances?

Chapter 113

What I learned: In God's eyes, a person's value has no relationship to wealth or position on the social ladder.

The question: Does the Bible quantify in any way how much time and money we should contribute to helping the poor?

Chapter 114

What I learned: To tremble at God's presence means to recognize God's complete power and authority and our frailty by comparison.

The question: How do non-Christians explain the many acts of nature that occur around us?

Chapter 115

What I learned: Today, we still may put more value in tangible objects (home, possessions, clothing, and money) than intangible realities (spiritual growth and time with others).

The question: What are the idols that we sinfully place before God in certain situations?

Chapter 116

What I learned: The psalmist asks to be saved after indicating that "the cords of death entangled me, the anguish of the grave came over me" (verse 3).

The question: What vows did the psalmist make to God that must be fulfilled for hearing the cry of the psalmist?

Chapter 117

What I learned: The shortest chapter in the Bible gives the message that God's salvation is for all people, not just the Jews.

The question: When giving praise to the Lord, what should Christians be most thankful for?

Chapter 118

What I learned: The Lord is my strength and my defense, and he has become my salvation.

The question: Does our trust in God fluctuate and dependent on context?

Chapter 119

What I learned: Everywhere we look we find temptation to fill our minds with thoughts of sexual relationships that God would not approve of.

The question: Can we make the claim that we love God's law, but repetitively commit the same sin?

Chapter 120

What I learned: All believers must live with the tension of being in the world but not belonging to it.

The question: When accused falsely as the psalmist was accused, should we defend against the accuser or just pray to God and not react?

Chapter 121

What I learned: As God protected the pilgrims on their journey to Jerusalem, God protects us in our day-to-day activities.

The question: Because of the crime and evil that takes place in the world, are there occasions when God chooses not to protect us?

Chapter 122

What I learned: Real peace comes through faith in God because he embodies all the characteristics of peace that the world cannot provide.

The question: How often should we involve ourselves in intercessory prayer as opposed to praying for God to fix our own weaknesses?

Chapter 123

What I learned: The psalmist asked God for mercy when being attacked by his enemies.

The question: Do we have the tendency to be impatient when asking God for mercy?

Chapter 124

What I learned: Not always realizing who our enemies may be, God delivers us from those who seek to destroy us.

The question: What causes people to believe that God does not have the ability to solve our country's problems?

Chapter 125

What I learned: Human sinfulness often ruin God's ideal on earth, but that doesn't mean that God has lost control because evil prevails only as long as God allows.

The question: What are reasons why God allows evil to prevail?

Chapter 126

What I learned: When burdened by sorrow, know that times of grief will end and that joy will again be found.

The question: How does God expect us to handle times of grief and sorrow?

Chapter 127

What I learned: We should not make the mistake of leaving God out of our lives because all of our accomplishments will be futile if we choose to do so.

The question: How do we get more families to have God as their foundation?

Chapter 128

What I learned: The values outlined in God's Word include love, service, honesty, integrity, and prayer, which helps all relationships.

The question: Which of these values should be given more time by Christians?

Chapter 129

What I learned: When we face persecution and discrimination, take courage because the church will never be destroyed.

The question: How do we take action to get strength to handle adversity in times of persecution?

Chapter 130

What I learned: God doesn't keep a record of our sins. When he forgives, he forgives completely by tearing down any wall between him and us.

The question: What are the sins that we ask for forgiveness for but often repeat? Is the sincerity of our forgiveness in question?

Chapter 131

What I learned: Humility puts others first and allows us to be content with God's leading in our lives.

The question: What does David mean when he states in verse 1, "I do not concern myself with great matters or things to wonderful for me"?

Chapter 132

What I learned: We must live so close to God that we become restless until God's will is accomplished through us.

The question: What amount of effort does it take to reach a point where we are restless until God's will is accomplished through us?

Chapter 133

What I learned: As Christians, we must agree on our purpose in life, which is to work together for God.

The question: What does it mean to be dedicated to serving God wholeheartedly?

Chapter 134

What I learned: We must honor God by the quality of our work and the attitude of service we bring to it.

The question: What jobs are available for Christians that don't require us to be physically present at the church?

Chapter 135

What I learned: We must choose our priorities carefully because we will take on the characteristics of whatever we worship.

The question: How do we differentiate idol worship from those materialistic items we really value?

Chapter 136

What I learned: The repetition of the phrase, "His love endures forever," allows for this important lesson to sink in.

The question: What would make us believe that God's love would run out?

Chapter 137

What I learned: The Edomites were related to the Israelites, but rejoiced when the Babylonians besieged Israel.

The question: Is asking God to take revenge different than wishing harm on our enemies?

Chapter 138

What I learned: "Though I walk in the midst of trouble, you preserve my life" (verse 7).

The question: How do we best include God's plan for our lives in our current and future plans?

Chapter 139

What I learned: If we ask the Lord to search our hearts and our thoughts and to reveal our sin, we will be continuing on God's "way everlasting" (verse 24)

The question: Should we invest prayer time into asking God to judge or harm our enemies?

Chapter 140

What I learned: "Keep me safe, Lord, from the hands of the wicked, protect me from the violent, who devises ways to trip my feet" (verse 4).

The question: Should we pray for protection every day (repetition), or does God already recognize our need for protection after a single prayer?

Chapter 141

What I learned: It isn't enough to ask God to keep us away from temptation, make us stronger, or change our circumstances; but ask to be changed in the inside.

The question: What role does constructive criticism have during sermons by church leaders?

Chapter 142

What I learned: "When my spirit grows faint within me, it is you who watch over my way" (verse 3).

The question: What is the difference between a complaint (as David indicated) and a concern?

Chapter 143

What I learned: At times, we may feel caught in deepening depression and are unable to pull ourselves out.

The question: As David was losing hope in his current situation, is it natural to expect God to answer us quickly?

Chapter 144

What I learned: Live for God—he alone can make our lives worthwhile, purposeful, and meaningful.

The question: Before we leave this earth, which actions does God expect us to complete?

Chapter 145

What I learned: Sometimes our burdens seem more than we can bear, and we wonder how we can go on.

The question: Does God expect us to handle some burdens and decide not to remove them regardless of prayer?

Chapter 146

What I learned: We shouldn't be surprised when others don't understand our Christian values, but don't give in to their values.

The question: Should more effort be exerted into convincing our family members to believe in God as opposed to strangers?

Chapter 147

What I learned: The more we learn about God and his ways, the better we will understand ourselves.

The question: How do atheists and agnostics explain the weather, types of animals, and the food they obtain?

Chapter 148

What I learned: Praise includes expressing admiration, appreciation, and thanks, but also just for knowing who God is.

The question: What actions should we engage in other than church fellowship to let others know what God he has done for us?

Chapter 149

What I learned: The double-edged sword represents the completeness of judgment that will be executed by the Messiah.

The question: Are there other options we should consider in praising God besides song and prayer?

Chapter 150

What I learned: If we choose God's way of life, we still face both blessings and troubles, joy and grief, and success and obstacles.

The question: How can we determine through peoples' actions that they are following the road toward God?

BOOK TWENTY

Proverbs

Chapter 1
What I learned: In making wise choices, we must steer clear (of objects) that may unintentionally entice us to sin when we know it is wrong.

The question: Do Christians truly believe that knowledge and wisdom is obtained through reading God's Word?

Chapter 2
What I learned: Two of the most difficult sins to resist are pride and sexual immorality, and we must ask God for the strength to avoid these temptations.

The question: Why does it appear that atheists have the wisdom to do some tasks that we aim to achieve?

Chapter 3
What I learned: The proverbs serve as general statements and are not guaranteed to prevent us from dealing with difficulties in life.

The question: When we face difficulties in life, do these occur due primarily to lack of wisdom or lack of faith?

Chapter 4
What I learned: "Hold on to instruction, do not let it go, guard it well, for it is your life" (verse 11).

The question: Who would God consider to be the wisest person living today?

Chapter 5
What I learned: There are many temptations that cause sexual immorality, which is against God's law and can destroy a family.

The question: What steps can we take to be completely free of sexual immorality?

Chapter 6

What I learned: "Do not lust in your heart after her beauty or let her captivate you with her eyes" (verse 25).

The question: Why is lusting so difficult for men to control?

Chapter 7

What I learned: To combat temptation, we must make sure that our lives are full of God's Word, and recognize the strategies of temptation and run fast from them.

The question: Are attending nightclubs as young men an invitation to sexual sin?

Chapter 8

What I learned: Harboring secret sins means that we are tolerating evil within ourselves.

The question: How was it determined that a woman is speaking in this chapter?

Chapter 9

What I learned: Wisdom appeals first to the mind, while folly appeals first to the senses, which is why we get sidetracked when looking for wisdom.

The question: How does God help us to decide when (and how) we should respond back to constructive criticism?

Chapter 10

What I learned: If we are righteous people (loving the Lord and seeking to follow him), we should not fear death, and look forward to eternal life.

The question: Are Christians ever given enough wisdom to understand why some experience exceptions from these proverbs?

Chapter 11

What I learned: Our perspectives and understanding is severely limited, so we must seek counsel and be open to advice.

The question: What does the psalmist mean when he states, "Whoever puts up security for a stranger will surely suffer, but whoever refuses to shake hands in pledge is safe" (verse 15)?

Chapter 12

What I learned: For many, death is a darkened door at the end of life, a passageway to an unknown and feared destiny.

The question: What methods does God use to help us deal with the fear of death?

Chapter 13

What I learned: "I was wrong" or "I need advice" are difficult phrases to offer because they require humility.

The question: How do we differentiate between criticism that brings us down and constructive criticism that represents good advice?

Chapter 14

What I learned: The right choice often requires hard work and self-sacrifice.

The question: Do we understand enough about why people are in poverty to best help them as God requires of us?

Chapter 15

What I learned: We cannot always choose what happens to us, but we can choose our actions toward these situations and our responses to them.

The question: Do we not have many advisors (as God would expect) because we are too prideful to ask for help?

Chapter 16

What I learned: In doing God's will, there must be a partnership between our efforts and God's control.

The question: As we build a better relationship with God, does God give us more control regarding our quality of life?

Chapter 17

What I learned: The benefits of remaining quiet are that it allows the opportunity to listen, to learn, and to gather wisdom from those who are wiser.

The question: Who is the psalmist referring to as "the messenger of death" (verse 11) who God sends against evildoers?

Chapter 18

What I learned: Three basic principles for making sound decisions are: (1) get the facts before answering, (2) be open to new ideas, and (3) and hear both sides before judging.

The question: What does God mean for the current day when he states, "Casting the lot settles disputes"?

Chapter 19

What I learned: A lower standard of living (even poverty) is a small price to pay for personal integrity.

The question: How does God define "lazy" when he states, "Laziness brings on deep sleep, and the shiftless goes hungry" (verse 15)?

Chapter 20

What I learned: As soon as we confess our sin and repent, sinful actions and thoughts creep back into our lives, which is why we need ongoing cleansing.

The question: Does God expect us to offer him any vows since they can be difficult not to break?

Chapter 21

What I learned: "The horse is made ready for the day of battle, but victory rests with the Lord" (verse 31).

The question: Is overcharging for products considered sinful (dishonest weights and dishonest scales)?

Chapter 22

What I learned: "Gerrymandering" means changing political boundaries so that one group of neighbors benefits and the other loses.

The question: How do we decide when it is best to speak up against unjust authoritarian employers?

Chapter 23

What I learned: The people most likely to gain knowledge are those who are willing to listen.

The question: How we tell that we are engaged in gluttony, a sin by God's standards?

Chapter 24

What I learned: We ought not complain about our problems since the problems we face today are training us for more difficult situations in the future.

The question: Does God promise that we will face problems in our future to strengthen our character and our faith?

Chapter 25

What I learned: Dwelling on what we should have received may make us miss the satisfaction of knowing we did our best.

The question: Since it is best to quietly and faithfully accomplish the work of God, is it inappropriate to say much about these accomplishments?

Chapter 26

What I learned: It is best to keep out of arguments that are none of our business unless we choose to intervene when the parties cool down.

The question: How much effort do we exert to the "fools" if the "fools" represent family members who don't take advice representing God's vision?

Chapter 27

What I learned: Because life is short and our fortunes uncertain, we should be more diligent in what we do with our lives.

The question: How often (if ever) should we thank God or praise ourselves for our accomplishments?

Chapter 28

What I learned: God does not listen to our prayers if we intend to go back to our sin as soon as we get off our knees.

The question: If God had to choose one task that we should do to help others, what would that task be?

Chapter 29

What I learned: When we refuse to accept valid criticism, we leave ourselves open to sudden disaster.

The question: When we recognize that there is a sin prevalent in our lives, why don't we quickly eliminate the sin?

Chapter 30

What I learned: Agar, a wise teacher, asked God not to refuse him before he died and to give him neither poverty or riches, but only his daily bread.

The question: What is meant by the statement, "[T]hose whose eyes are ever so haughty, whose glances are so disdainful" (verse 13)?

Chapter 31

What I learned: Proverbs is very practical for our day because it shows us how to become wise, make good decisions, and live by God's ideal.

The question: What role does the husband have for teaching his wife about God's idea of a wife of noble character?

BOOK TWENTY-ONE

Ecclesiastes

Chapter 1

What I learned: All human accomplishments will one day disappear, so only the pursuit of God will provide lifelong satisfaction.

The question: Can we maximize our serving of God's kingdom while maintaining a busy lifestyle? In what ways?

Chapter 2

What I learned: We must look beyond our activities to the reasons we do them and the purpose they fulfill, as well as the role God plays.

The question: Are most of the activities we do in life done to please God, please others, or please ourselves?

Chapter 3

What I learned: We can best understand our purpose in life by building a relationship with God, fearing him, and seeking his guidance.

The question: What does God want us to understand in preparation for the next life?

Chapter 4

What I learned: Take time to enjoy the other gifts God has given, and realize that it is God who gives out the assignments and rewards, not us.

The question: How does we know when it is best to seek companions and when it is best to figure out problems on our own?

Chapter 5

What I learned: We can be content with what we have when we realize that with God, we have everything we need.

The question: Does God have a greater concern more about peoples' weath or the methods in which they attain wealth?

Chapter 6

What I learned: Many people work hard to improve their physical condition to prolong life, but the same effort is not given to improve spiritual health.

The question: What does Solomon mean when he states that a man "may not enjoy his prosperity and a proper burial" (verse 3)?

Chapter 7

What I learned: Death reminds us that we still have time to change, time to examine the direction in our lives, and time to confess our sins since life is short.

The question: Although suffering can refine us and help us grow, isn't it natural to pray to God for an avoidance of suffering?

Chapter 8

What I learned: Wisdom (respect and honor for God) is the ability to see life from God's perspective, and then to know the best course of action to take.

The question: Does God share with us why the righteous get what the wicked deserve and why the wicked get what the righteous deserve?

Chapter 9

What I learned: Life can be unfair, the world is finite, and sin has twisted life, making it what God did not intend.

The question: Because the future is uncertain, can we understand the impact of sin on our future?

Chapter 10

What I learned: In each situation, "sharpening the ax" means recognizing where a problem exists, acquiring or honing the skills to do the job better, and then going out and doing it.

The question: What skills do we need to sharpen to serve God at a higher capacity?

Chapter 11

What I learned: We need a spirit of trust and adventure, facing life's risks and opportunities with God-directed enthusiasm and faith.

The question: If Christians will be with God for eternity, then why are we so fearful of death?

Chapter 12

What I learned: A life centered around God will make "days of trouble" (verse 1) (sickness, disabilities, and handicaps) fulfilling because of the hope of eternal life.

The question: When God judges us at death (and while on earth), does God reduce punishment for confession and repentance of sins?

BOOK TWENTY-TWO

Song of Songs

Chapter 1
What I learned: The girl (Solomon's lover) felt insecure because of her dark skin, which was different from the other Israelite girls.

The question: Was outward beauty the original reason why Solomon chose this girl to marry?

Chapter 2
What I learned: The "little foxes" (verse 15) (small problems that can destroy a relationship) can rise to larger problems and must not be ignored or minimized.

The question: How can younger Christians properly develop a love relationship without concerns of lust and intimacy?

Chapter 3
What I learned: The first few verses remind us about the willingness to sacrifice our personal comfort for the ones we love.

The question: When reading Scripture, how can we tell the difference between a dream and actions that happen in reality?

Chapter 4
What I learned: Partners in marriage should continually work at refreshing each other by an encouraging word or withholding a discussion of a problem.

The question: Did Solomon truly believe that his bride had no flaws?

Chapter 5
What I learned: Two married people should also be best friends, which involves listening, sharing, and showing understanding for the other's likes and dislikes.

The question: How can we tell through this poem that the relationship between Solomon and his bride had problems?

Chapter 6

What I learned: Polygamy, although not condoned, was common in Old Testament days, which means that Solomon always had other wives and concubines available.

The question: Why did God allow polygamy to be so prevalent in the Old Testament although he wanted marriage to be more sacred?

Chapter 7

What I learned: Solomon compared body parts to beautiful objects of nature.

The question: How should Christians describe the beauty of their lovers? Should other comparisons be made to things/people besides objects?

Chapter 8

What I learned: Solomon's bride was able to stand strong in the face of sexual temptation.

The question: Why were breasts and the use of the word "pomegranate" (verse 2) used often in the Song of Songs?

BOOK TWENTY-THREE

Isaiah

Chapter 1

What I learned: The Israelites placed more faith in the rituals of their religion (sacrifice and offerings) than in the God they worshipped.

The question: What were the reasons why the Israelites continued to sin despite God's warnings to them?

Chapter 2

What I learned: The day of judgment will come, and we will need to have a proper relationship with God when it comes.

The question: What does it mean to have a proper relationship with God to the extent that God is very pleased with us?

Chapter 3

What I learned: When God blesses us with money or position, don't flaunt it, but use what we have to help others, not impress them.

The question: Are the wicked described here those people who sin openly with no regard for God and are unapologetic?

Chapter 4

What I learned: Holiness comes from a sincere desire to obey God's moral standards and wholehearted devotion to God.

The question: Can we obtain some understanding as to why God protects some Christians from evil but not others?

Chapter 5

What I learned: God condemns six sins: (1) exploiting others, (2) drunkenness, (3) taking sarcastic pride in sin, (4) confusing moral standards, (5) being conceited, and (6) perverting justice.

The question: What can be done to convince people who are involved in these sins that they are morally wrong according to God's standards?

Chapter 6

What I learned: When we recognize how great God is, how sinful we are, and the extent of God's forgiveness, we receive power to do his work.

The question: As with Judith, is it expected that when preachers (or other Christians) speak to a secular audience that very few people listen?

Chapter 7

What I learned: In this chapter, "virgin" is translated from a Hebrew word used for an unmarried woman old enough to be married—one who is sexually mature.

The question: Does there come a point where God runs out of patience with our continuous sinning and destroys us as he did with the city of Israel?

Chapter 8

What I learned: Fear is a powerful enemy of our faith and a strong deterrent to believers' peace of mind, so we must trust in God to minimize these fears.

The question: Does our limited knowledge affect our trust in God because we can't always understand why things happen to us?

Chapter 9

What I learned: Too often we take pride in our accomplishments, forgetting that it is God who has given us our every resource and ability.

The question: How does God want us to differentiate between confidence in our abilities and being prideful?

Chapter 10

What I learned: The key to being a true Christian is faith in God and understanding that we are only useful to the extent we allow God to use us.

The question: Without a historical overview of the conquered cities, will we struggle in understanding the meaning of these passages?

Chapter 11

What I learned: The righteousness that God values is more than just refraining from sin, but actively offering help to others (especially the poor).

The question: What does the first coming of Christ mean in Scripture?

Chapter 12

What I learned: We should express our gratitude to God by thinking him, praising him, and spreading the good news to others.

The question: What impacts why Christians don't spread the gospel more often?

Chapter 13

What I learned: Babylon, a symbol of God's enemies, was located in present-day Iraq, was never inhabited, and is buried under mounds of dirt and sand.

The question: Are many of the inhabitants of Iraq still enemies of Christians and Jesus Christ?

Chapter 14

What I learned: Beware of placing confidence in human power because one day it will fade, no matter how strong it appears now.

The question: Since pride willfully opposes God and will result in judgment, what must we do as Christians to eliminate pride from our lives?

Chapter 15

What I learned: An enemy of Israel, Moab, will be punished by God for treating Israel harshly.

The question: Would God place this type of punishment on a group of people who hate Christians as was done in biblical times?

Chapter 16

What I learned: When we seek our own ways in order to get through our daily troubles, there is no effect unless we rely on God.

The question: Do we, as a country, rely on God to help us in times of trouble?

Chapter 17

What I learned: Be on the alert for how sexual images divert us from God since the media and entertainment feed our obsession for sex.

The question: Since our world and society show so many sexual images, how do we respond when seeing these images?

Chapter 18

What I learned: We can have the tendency to trust in government, science, education, medical care, and financial systems before trusting in God.

The question: How do we best add God's role into these systems?

Chapter 19

What I learned: We must ask God for wisdom to guide our decisions or we will also be uncertain and misdirected.

The question: Are there countries today that are expected to receive punishment like Egypt?

Chapter 20

What I learned: God asked Isaiah to walk naked for about three years to represent the humiliation of Egypt and Cush, which seemed illogical.

The question: Does it represent a lack of faith if we question what God asks us to do?

Chapter 21

What I learned: Babylon was a great and powerful city known for its horrible sins and remains a symbol of all that stands against God.

The question: What is meant in verse 2 in the prophecy against Babylon, "Media, lay siege"?

Chapter 22

What I learned: There are two common responses to hopelessness: despair and self-indulgence, but we must not act as if there is no hope because there is another life.

The question: Why did God put his servant in a "firm" (verse 25) place, and then allow him to fall?

Chapter 23

What I learned: Unlike the people of Tyre who suffered from pride, we must examine our lives and remember that all true accomplishments come from God.

The question: Did the evil embedded in Tyre result from their great wealth?

Chapter 24

What I learned: Sin affects every aspect of society so extensively that even those faithful to God suffer due to human sin.

The question: When we try to minimize sin that is rampant, would God prefer we work on our own sins or the sins of others?

Chapter 25

What I learned: We should think of the prayers God has answered and praise him for his goodness and faithfulness.

The question: What are the differences between those who oppose God (Moab) and those who don't believe in God's existence?

Chapter 26

What I learned: Instead of trying to hide our shameful thoughts and actions from God, confess them to him and receive his forgiveness.

The question: What is it that we can understand from the Bible regarding life after death?

Chapter 27

What I learned: God indicates that he is dealing with a people with no understanding, so he has no compassion on them and shows them no favor.

The question: Are there occasions that God gives us no compassion or favor if we continue to sin?

Chapter 28

What I learned: As God did with Israel, God takes all our individual circumstances and weaknesses into account and deals with us sensitively.

The question: What does God mean by the phrase, "Do this, do that, a rule for this, a rule for that, a little here, a little there" (verse 10)?

Chapter 29

What I learned: Often we slip into routine patterns when we worship, and we neglect to give God our love and devotion.

The question: What are the "siege works" (verse 3) that God stated he set up on Israel?

Chapter 30

What I learned: The next time we go through a difficult time, try to appreciate the experience and grow through it, learning what God wants to teach us.

The question: Other than prayer, what other actions does God want us to take when dealing with adversity or difficult situations?

Chapter 31

What I learned: The Israelites did not want to pay the price of looking to God and repenting of their sinful ways and instead chose to turn primarily to human help.

The question: Since we naturally make decisions without prayer, how do people decide when it is best to ask for God's help?

Chapter 32

What I learned: When Jesus Christ reigns in our hearts, there is no place for sin, no matter how well hidden we may think it is.

The question: What are some of these hidden sins that generally affect Christians? Why are they so difficult to eliminate from Christian lives?

Chapter 33

What I learned: If we are fair and honest in our relationships, we will dwell with God, and he will supply our needs.

The question: Does God handle different types of sinners (the Assyrians and modern-day Christians) in different manners?

Chapter 34

What I learned: Prophecy predicts and history reveals what has been in God's mind for all time.

The question: What does God mean by "all the starry host will fall" (verse 4)?

Chapter 35

What I learned: "And a highway will be there; it will be called the Way of Holiness; it will be for those who walk on that Way" (verse 8).

The question: Is the "Way of Holiness" an actual road or a figurative representation of a Christian's journey for those who follow God?

Chapter 36

What I learned: People don't necessarily need to be sinful to be ineffective for God; they need only be confused about what God wants.

The question: What is some common human advice given to us that goes against God's Word but difficult to turn away from?

Chapter 37

What I learned: God is prepared to do the impossible if we trust him to ask and have faith that the task can be accomplished.

The question: In trying to understand faith, will there always be a conflict between the evidence shown in our world and God's Word?

Chapter 38

What I learned: When Hezekiah prayed to the Lord after he became very ill, the Lord added fifteen years to Hezekiah's life.

The question: Did he (Hezekiah's) faith in God need to be very high to receive a blessing of this magnitude?

Chapter 39

What I learned: Hezekiah showed all his treasures to a prince of Babylon although Hezekiah was warned not to trust Babylon, who would destroy Judah.

The question: When Hezekiah showed the Babylonian prince his treasures, was this intentional due to pride or unintentional by just showing gratitude?

Chapter 40

What I learned: "Even youth grow tired and weary and young men stumble and fall, but those who hope in the Lord will renew their strength" (verses 30–31).

The question: When we doubt God's promises, do we have a lack of confidence in God's ability or a lack of confidence in ourselves?

Chapter 41

What I learned: We need not fear because (1) God is with us, (2) God has established a relationship with us, and (3) God gives us assurance of his victory over sin and death.

The question: Does God expect us to have no fear in every circumstance?

Chapter 42

What I learned: Sometimes partial blindness—seeing but not understanding, or knowing what is right but not doing it—can be worse than not seeing at all.

The question: What is meant by the verse, "For a long time, I kept silent, I have been quiet and held myself back, but now like a woman in childbirth, I cry out, I gasp and pant" (verse 14)?

Chapter 43

What I learned: Because believers today should share the responsibility of being God's witnesses, we should show what God is like through our words and examples.

The question: How often (and in what capacity) should we be witnessing for God?

Chapter 44

What I learned: We think of idols and statues of wood and stone, but an idol is anything that is given sacred value and power.

The question: How can we determine if we idolize money, power, or prestige?

Chapter 45

What I learned: When bad times come, we shouldn't resent them, but instead ask what we can learn from these experiences to make us better servants.

The question: Why does the Lord specifically refer to Cyrus as anointed as compared to other prophets who did special tasks for God?

Chapter 46

What I learned: Much of the book of Isaiah speaks of a future deliverance when we will all live with God in perfect peace.

The question: If there is perfect peace after death for Christians, why do people want to remain on earth when they may be near death?

Chapter 47

What I learned: We must look at our own lives, and ask ourselves how we can be more responsible with the talents and possessions God has given us.

The question: Can a person be both a Christian and a sorcerer/astrologer?

Chapter 48

What I learned: Many people cry out for comfort, security, and relief, but they haven't taken the first steps to turn away from sin and open up to God.

The question: Can a Christian have strong faith and a strong relationship with God and have minimal suffering?

Chapter 49

What I learned: Christians must play a stronger role through social media to spread the gospel around the world.

The question: When we do suffer for lengthy periods of time, why would Christians believe that God has forsaken them?

Chapter 50

What I learned: When we place confidence in our own intelligence, appearance, or accomplishments instead of in God, we can risk torment later.

The question: Are there specific reasons why God may choose not to fight for us?

Chapter 51

What I learned: The Israelites had a reason to fear Babylon due to potential harm, but they should have realized and believed that God's power is greater than Babylon's.

The question: Do people tend not to believe God and his message of salvation due to lack of visual evidence?

Chapter 52

What I learned: We are expected to share the good news of redemption, salvation, and peace with others.

The question: Should more time be invested in sharing God's news with other Christians or with non-Christians?

Chapter 53

What I learned: "We all, like sheep, have gone astray, each of us has turned to our own way, and the Lord has laid on him the iniquity of us all" (verse 6).

The question: Do we have to pray continuously due to the fact that we can't always meet God's standards and show our appreciation for God?

Chapter 54

What I learned: Sin separates us from God and brings us pain and suffering, but if we confess our sin and repent, God will forgive us.

The question: Did God give the possibility of abandoning us based on our behavior, "For a brief moment I abandoned you, but will bring you back with compassion" (verse 7)?

Chapter 55

What I learned: We must come, seek, listen, and call on God and must eagerly receive God's free nourishment.

The question: What must we do as Christians to understand some of God's thoughts and purposes since his thoughts are not our thoughts?

Chapter 56

What I learned: A day where we rest and focus on God (Sabbath) is held by Christians either on Saturday or Sunday.

The question: Is it considered a sin to work seven days a week (other than nonpaid church-related work) since a full day is not given to God?

Chapter 57

What I learned: We cannot gain our salvation through good deeds because our best deeds are not good enough to outweigh our sins.

The question: Did God give the perception that these idols have power to test the Israelites' commitment to God?

Chapter 58

What I learned: Our faith may lack sincerity if it doesn't reach out to others.

The question: How often does God expect us to fast? Is there a preferred method that God wants us to fast?

Chapter 59

What I learned: "For our offenses are many in your sight, and our sins testify against us" (verse 12).

The question: Does God punish us for sins we commit that we don't recognize since we would not confess those sins to God?

Chapter 60

What I learned: We long for the fulfillment of the future kingdom, but we must wait for God's timing.

The question: Do we have any control on God's timing of events in our lives?

Chapter 61

What I learned: We suffer for many reasons—our own mistakes, someone else's mistakes, and injustice—but God will reward those who suffer because of injustice.

The question: Can we play a role in minimizing suffering that is out of our control?

Chapter 62

What I learned: Isaiah prayed intensely and without resting for Israel to be saved and for God's will to be done.

The question: Should we repeatedly pray for the same thing or assume God already heard the first prayer?

Chapter 63

What I learned: Isaiah asked God for two favors: to show tenderness and compassion to the faithful remnant of Israel and to punish their enemies.

The question: Are atheists and agnostics considered God's enemies or our enemies? Who does God define as "our enemies" (verse 18)?

Chapter 64

What I learned: Our best efforts are still infected with sin, so our only hope is faith in Jesus who can cleanse us and bring us into God's presence.

The question: Does more faith in God generally lead to more mercy from God?

Chapter 65

What I learned: God gives us a pictoral description of the new heaven and new earth where there will be no more weeping and crying.

The question: Why do Christians fear dying if we believe we are going to heaven and will be in no more pain?

Chapter 66

What I learned: We can be just as negligent to feed the hungry, work for justice, obey God's Word, and take up God's causes as the Israelites were.

The question: How do Christians maintain an approved balance (from God) between God's work for us and our vocational work?

BOOK TWENTY-FOUR

Jeremiah

Chapter 1

What I learned: Jeremiah had strong faith in God to the point where he continued to share God's law and very few listened to him.

The question: How do Christians maintain an approved balance (from God) between God's work for us and our vocational work?

Chapter 2

What I learned: The Israelites got so comfortable in their sin that they could not think of giving it up, which is a likely sign of addiction.

The question: Does God put value into recognition of sin (with attempts to correct the sin) even if the sin continues?

Chapter 3

What I learned: If we view every wrong attitude and action as a serious offense against God, we will begin to understand what living for God is all about.

The question: Can Christians be truly repentant toward a particular sin if we go back and commit the same sin?

Chapter 4

What I learned: Old habits and hidden sins must be uprooted and rejected if we expect God's Word to take root and grow in our life.

The question: What are examples of hidden sins within Christian living?

Chapter 5

What I learned: Don't wait until God removes our cherished resources before committing ourselves to him as we should.

The question: What are the different options that Christians do to help the fatherless and the poor?

Chapter 6

What I learned: We should take time to confess our sins to God, reflect on the areas of our lives that he has already refined, then thank God for what he is doing in our lives.

The question: How do we inform others of their sins? Have those people been receptive to constructive criticism without being judged?

Chapter 7

What I learned: Many think that religious affiliation will protect us from evil and problems and try to only maintain the "image" of being a Christian.

The question: What should we understand about different levels of sacrifice to God and how these levels impact living for God?

Chapter 8

What I learned: Some of the Israelites were living sinful lives by choice, deceiving themselves that there would be no consequences and lost perspective.

The question: Are we just as guilty as the Israelites in not fully understanding all of God's requirements as Christians?

Chapter 9

What I learned: God put a higher priority on knowing him personally and living a life that reflects his justice, righteousness, and love.

The question: How does our continuous sinning differ from those of the Israelites?

Chapter 10

What I learned: "Discipline me, Lord, but only in due measure, not in your anger, or you will reduce me to nothing" (verse 24).

The question: Is the degree of discipline given to us impacted by a combination of type of sin, prayer, relationship with God, and confession?

Chapter 11

What I learned: There may come a point where God must dispense justice and will not answer prayers.

The question: Are there still people today that worship multiple gods made of carved wood and stone?

Chapter 12

What I learned: God makes a powerful statement when he says, "My inheritance has become to me like a lion in the forest, she roars at me, therefore, I hate her"(verse 8).

The question: Can we have the tendency to misinterpret God's answers and responses as not being heard if situations get worse?

Chapter 13

What I learned: Our attitudes and patterns for living can become so set that we lose all desire to change and will no longer fear the consequences.

The question: Did the people of Judah need more visual images such as the linen belt in order to believe and listen to God?

Chapter 14

What I learned: God rejected the prayers of Judah because they chose not to repent and listened to false prophets who told them what they wanted to hear.

The question: Why, in many cases, do we choose to do what is wrong when we know what is right?

Chapter 15

What I learned: Three important messages from this chapter are: (1) in prayer, we can reveal our deepest thoughts to God; (2) God expects us to trust him; and (3) we should influence others for God.

The question: When we get angry, hurt, and afraid like Jeremiah, are we ever in a position to accuse God of not helping us?

Chapter 16

What I learned: The first step of repentance is to acknowledge God knows about our sins.

The question: Was the worshipping of idols by the Israelites a "greater" sin or not recognizing and repenting a "greater" sin?

Chapter 17

What I learned: God makes it clear why we sin—it is a matter of the heart because our hearts were inclined to sin from the day we were born.

The question: What are methods we can use to resist the temptation to sin?

Chapter 18

What I learned: When we are being criticized, we should listen carefully because God may be trying to tell us something.

The question: Is Jeremiah's plea to ask God not to forgive the crimes of the Israelites appropriate here?

Chapter 19

What I learned: Food became so scarce in Jerusalem due to the sins of the Israelites that they became cannibals, where some ate their own children.

The question: What was the key moment when God said that he would no longer forgive the Israelites and execute judgment?

Chapter 20

What I learned: If someone with such intimate awareness of God's presence, such as Jeremiah, struggled with insecurities, we should not be surprised by our failures.

The question: What are some of the similarities and differences between how Jeremiah and Job handled adversity?

Chapter 21

What I learned: Too often we expect God to help us in our time of trouble even though we have ignored him in our time of prosperity.

The question: Was there any remnant of Israelites who followed God's laws, or did the Lord decide that everyone would suffer or die?

Chapter 22

What I learned: Events that occur in the Bible are not necessarily in chronological order (events in chapter 22 occurred before events in chapter 21).

The question: Why did God tell the people of Judah not to mourn for the good King Josiah but to mourn for the evil exiled King Jehoahaz?

Chapter 23

What I learned: We may reject a message or make fun of it because it would require us to change our ways.

The question: Do people choose not to share the gospel because of greater responsibility or a perceived lack of knowledge and confidence?

Chapter 24

What I learned: Trouble is a blessing if it makes us stronger, and prosperity is a curse if it entices us away from God.

The question: Did the Israelites have a choice as to whether they would be exiled to Babylon, and did it challenge the faith of those who were exiled?

Chapter 25

What I learned: Jeremiah preached the same message for twenty-three years asking the people of Judah to turn to God, but they still would not listen.

The question: Do we deserve the same punishment as the people of Judah because we continue to sin as Christians even when told by God and his messengers?

Chapter 26

What I learned: God reminded Jeremiah to give his entire message no matter how uncomfortable it made Jeremiah or how the people of Judah felt.

The question: Although Uriah gave a prophecy similar to that of Jeremiah, was he executed because he fled in fear to Egypt?

Chapter 27

What I learned: God informed the people of Judah to either serve the foreign ruler Nebuchadnezzar or die by the sword.

The question: Do the false prophets of biblical times and current times actually admit to being false prophets?

Chapter 28

What I learned: People still prefer to listen to temporary comforting lies than painful long-lasting truth.

The question: Why did Jeremiah agree with the false prophet Hananiah that relief would come in two years when he knew these words are not from God?

Chapter 29

What I learned: When we enter times of trouble or sudden change, pray diligently and move ahead rather than giving up because of fear and uncertainty.

The question: What are some of the common lies and false prophecies told by these false prophets in today's time?

Chapter 30

What I learned: Sinful people cannot be cured by being good or being religious, but by allowing God to cure the disease of sin.

The question: Along with prayer, what can we do to eliminate our sins?

Chapter 31

What I learned: The old covenant, broken by the people, would be replaced with a new covenant with Jesus as the new foundation.

The question: Does this chapter have some similarities on what it will be like in heaven?

Chapter 32

What I learned: It isn't easy for us to believe that God can fulfill his "impossible" promises, but we must trust him regardless.

The question: What is the contradiction between verse 18 ("children are punished for the sins of their parents") and verse 19 ("you are rewarded according to your conduct")?

Chapter 33

What I learned: Surely God could take care of our needs without asking, but when we ask, we are acknowledging that we cannot accomplish our needs in our own strength.

The question: Does the Bible state how often we should pray to God to maintain peace and prosperity?

Chapter 34

What I learned: After God informed King Zedekiah that he would die peacefully instead of dying by the sword, the people of Judah returned to their sins.

The question: Can we also be guilty of returning to our sinful ways when the Lord blesses us or gives us relief that we don't deserve?

Chapter 35

What I learned: The Rekabites were steadfast in their commitment to their forefather Jehonadab to not drink wine, but the people of Israel disobeyed for years.

The question: Why did the Rekabites include in their vow never to build houses, sow seed, or plant vineyards and to live as nomads?

Chapter 36

What I learned: Speaking out against ungodly actions takes courage, which means that anyone who lives for God must stand for what is right even if others turn away.

The question: Are Christians who are strong in their faith often those who are willing to fight for God in strong opposition?

Chapter 37

What I learned: King Zedekiah wanted the blessings of his prayers from God that would not cost him anything.

The question: Do we need to rise to the level of sacrifice that Jeremiah did (being beaten and thrown into prison) to receive more blessings from God?

Chapter 38

What I learned: King Zedekiah couldn't decide between public opinion and God's will and tried to please everyone.

The question: Is it difficult to understand the concept that all of our blessings will not be given to us here on earth?

Chapter 39

What I learned: Eled-Melek was one of the few people saved during the fall of Jerusalem for trusting in the Lord and rescuing Jeremiah.

The question: Since we do not receive all of our blessings in this life, does God give blessings when we are in heaven?

Chapter 40

What I learned: Although Jeremiah was given the opportunity to go to Babylon to have great comfort and power, he chose to stay in "poor" Judah.

The question: Although Gedaliah was nice to Jeremiah as the appointed governor of Judah, did God allow his assassination because he didn't know him?

Chapter 41

What I learned: Without a king, with no law and no loyalty to God, Ishmael, who assassinated others, subjected Judah to complete anarchy.

The question: Who was Johanan, son of Kareah, who chased away Ishmael and recovered the captives held by Ishmael?

Chapter 42

What I learned: We should be sure never to ask God for something that we know in our hearts we really do not want.

The question: What was the temptation that the Israelites had to go to Egypt as opposed to staying with Judah as God commanded?

Chapter 43

What I learned: A recurring problem for most of us is seeking God's approval of our desires rather than asking God for guidance.

The question: Why may we be afraid to listen to God and choose to disobey him?

Chapter 44

What I learned: The wives of Judah credited idol worship because they had plenty of food, were well-off, and suffered no harm.

The question: Is it natural to run to places of comfort and security even when God may command us to take risks and suffer for him?

Chapter 45

What I learned: When we serve God, beware of focusing on what we are giving up, and ask God for forgiveness when this occurs.

The question: What was the strength of the relationship that Baruch (the scroll writer for Jeremiah) had with Jeremiah and God?

Chapter 46

What I learned: God punishes us to correct us and purify us, and although we don't want punishment, we should welcome its results.

The question: What can we do to minimize the severity of our punishments (other than prayer) when we sin intentionally?

Chapter 47

What I learned: The Philistines and the Israelites battled constantly, and the Lord decided to destroy the Philistines.

The question: Were the Philistines destroyed because of intentional violations of God's laws or because of how they treated the Israelites?

Chapter 48

What I learned: Moab was a very prideful city and convinced the Israelites to engage in idol worship, which were reasons that God destroyed Moab.

The question: Why did God state that he would restore Moab's fortunes in days to come?

Chapter 49

What I learned: God executed his judgment on many places (and tribes), which included Ammon, Edom, Damascus, Kedar, Hazor, and Elam.

The question: How did God decide which places would be desolate forever and which places he would eventually restore?

Chapter 50

What I learned: Getting rid of pride is not easy, but we can admit that it often rules us and ask God to forgive us and help us overcome it.

The question: Does pride play a role in the many wars that we have that may kill innocent people?

Chapter 51

What I learned: The wicked may succeed for a while, but resist the temptation to follow them or we may share in their judgment.

The question: Why did the Lord use so many methods to destroy Babylon?

Chapter 52

What I learned: As Jeremiah predicted the fall of Jerusalem, he was successful because God measures success by obedience, faithfulness, and righteousness.

The question: Do the poor people that Babylon spared to work the vineyards and fields represent believers in Christ?

BOOK TWENTY-FIVE

Lamentations

Chapter 1

What I learned: This chapter represents Jeremiah's song regarding the destruction of the nation of Judah for its refusal of following God's laws.

The question: Is it wrong not to weep for others as Jeremiah did for the Israelites?

Chapter 2

What I learned: Sinful people brought destruction on themselves, but tragically, sin's consequences affect everyone, good and evil alike.

The question: Do we occasionally pray for help that we don't believe will come or express love to God that we don't really have?

Chapter 3

What I learned: Bearing the yoke involves (1) silent reflection on what God wants, (2) repentant humility, (3) self-control in adversity, and (4) confident patience.

The question: When we complain about punishment for our sins, are we more concerned about not being forgiven for the sin or the impact resulting from the sin?

Chapter 4

What I learned: Life became so harsh that people even ate their own children, and dead bodies were left to rot in the street.

The question: How does God's punishment for doing evil differ between biblical times and the current time?

Chapter 5

What I learned: A lack of continual gratefulness to God often indicates that we are taking the goodness of life for granted.

The question: Should we talk God during prayer more about changing our own hearts or the hearts of others?

BOOK TWENTY-SIX

Ezekiel

Chapter 1
What I learned: God communicated with Ezekiel through apocalyptic imagery, which was used to convey ideas through symbolic pictures.

The question: Do experts have a definite understanding of what these symbols really represent, or do they use reasonable interpretations?

Chapter 2
What I learned: God will not judge us on how well others respond to our witness of our faith, but for how faithful we have been.

The question: When Ezekiel said, "The spirit came in to me and raise me"(verse 2), do actions like these still take place today? How is it explained?

Chapter 3
What I learned: God's message must sink deep into our hearts and show in our actions before we can effectively help others understand and apply the gospel.

The question: Should we invest more time in reaching out to nonbelievers, or should we help those Christians who know him but still disobey?

Chapter 4
What I learned: God had Ezekiel lay on his side for three hundred sixty days representing punishment for the Israelites and forty days for Judah (in years).

The question: Can we be as bold as Ezekiel to tell God to reconsider his actions (not to use human excrement for fuel, but cow dung instead)?

Chapter 5

What I learned: Too many people ignore God's warnings and treat them as empty threats.

The question: Why did God decide to keep a remnant of people who weren't really genuinely faithful to God?

Chapter 6

What I learned: God sometimes has to break people in order to bring them to true repentance.

The question: Are we truly repentant about a sin if we repeat the sin?

Chapter 7

What I learned: It is tragic that we spend so much money seeking to satisfy ourselves, and so little time seeking God, the true source of satisfaction.

The question: Why was the nation of Judah so attracted to making and worshiping idols?

Chapter 8

What I learned: God showed Ezekiel through a vision the detestable practices that the leaders of Israel were doing behind closed doors.

The question: Does God view sins behind closed doors differently from sins known to the public and others?

Chapter 9

What I learned: People have many convenient explanations to make it easier to sin such as, "It doesn't matter"; "everybody's doing it"; and "nobody will ever know."

The question: Who were the six men assigned to kill all those in Israel (except those with the mark), or was this a visual representation?

Chapter 10

What I learned: We must commit ourselves, our families, our churches, and our nation to follow God faithfully so that God does not abandon us.

The question: How much can we understand about the cherubim and the "man clothed in linen" (verse 2)?

Chapter 11

What I learned: The only effective way to deal with sin is to confess and ask God to help us overcome it.

The question: Did the Jews believe that God was not present everywhere but only primarily in the temple?

Chapter 12

What I learned: The Israelites did not believe all of the visions of destruction and punishment that was expected to come to them.

The question: What does the idea of Christ's return mean for us today?

Chapter 13

What I learned: False prophets gave visions that were not from God.

The question: Where do we currently see examples of false prophets in the church? How are they recognized?

Chapter 14

What I learned: We have idols in our hearts when we pursue reputation, acceptance, wealth, or sensual pleasure with the intensity that should be reserved for serving God.

The question: How often do our own sins result in our own punishment as opposed to the sins of others?

Chapter 15

What I learned: The people of Jerusalem were useless to God because of their idol worship, and so they would be destroyed and their cities burned.

The question: Are we doing enough as Christians to build the kingdom of God? What defines "enough"?

Chapter 16

What I learned: As we become wiser and more mature, we shouldn't turn away from the one who truly loves us.

The question: Why are sexual sins such as lust, adultery, and prostitution so likely to occur amongst people?

Chapter 17

What I learned: Although many miles apart, both Ezekiel and Jeremiah gave the same message to Jerusalem, which was not to be an ally with Egypt and trust in God.

The question: Should we also consider the use of allegories and parables to send messages to other people regarding God's Word?

Chapter 18

What I learned: Although we often suffer from the effects of sins committed by those who came before us, God does not punish us for someone else's sins.

The question: Are we truly repentant (as God demands) if we recognize the sin without completely removing the sin?

Chapter 19

What I learned: Ezekiel gave a lament to the people of Judah indicating that no kings of Judah would have the power to stop the destruction of Judah.

The question: Were both the people of Judah and the people of Israel in Babylon during the exile?

Chapter 20

What I learned: As the Israelites just considered God as another god, we must also be careful not to try to keep God pleased while also pursuing the pleasures the pleasures of sin.

The question: What are laws that we read in the Bible that Christians have the tendency to misinterpret, like the Israelites did with the dedication of firstborns?

Chapter 21

What I learned: Destruction is often a necessary part of purification, which occurred to the Israelites.

The question: How did Ezekiel feel about God's command of marking off a road so his people would be destroyed?

Chapter 22

What I learned: Don't use religion as a whitewash, but instead we must repair our lives by applying the principles of God's Word.

The question: Do the decisions of our leaders (if not God directed) punish us even if we did not commit the sin ourselves?

Chapter 23

What I learned: God punished Israel and Judah because they lusted after the Assyrians with lewdness and promiscuity and defiled themselves with the Assyrian idols.

The question: Why are sexual sins so difficult to overcome both in biblical times as well as today?

Chapter 24

What I learned: God told Ezekiel that his wife would die and instructed that Ezekiel was not to mourn for her to represent God's relationship with the people.

The question: Is there any reference that Ezekiel's wife played any role in her own death?

Chapter 25

What I learned: Ammon, Moab, Edom, and Philistia had once united with Judah, but not were punished as enemies of Judah.

The question: Do we currently have foreign nations like Judah's enemies that sin against God?

Chapter 26

What I learned: Tyre was destroyed because the city gloated over the destruction of Jerusalem and hoped to prosper and take all the trade routes Judah had.

The question: When the Bible discusses the destruction of foreign nations, are these nations evil because of the leaders or the inhabitants?

Chapter 27

What I learned: The beauty of Tyre was the source of its pride, and Tyre's pride guaranteed its judgment.

The question: Where is the line between arrogance and letting others know of our accomplishments?

Chapter 28

What I learned: The King of Tyre had so much pride that he thought (through his spiritual king, Satan) that he was a god.

The question: Is it fair to say that we will not be completely safe from harm in this life?

Chapter 29

What I learned: We have put forth a lot of hard work, but God supplied the resources, gave us the abilities, and provide us the opportunities for blessings.

The question: Did God feel disrespected by Egypt for not acknowledging his creations? Are we also guilty of this sin?

Chapter 30

What I learned: God allows nations (such as Babylon) to rise for a particular purpose, so we must pray that God's purpose will be carried out.

The question: When these wars occur between countries and kill innocent people, can we have a true understanding of God's purpose?

Chapter 31

What I learned: Egypt also took pride in its strength and beauty, then was ultimately cut down like a mighty tree.

The question: When God destroys a nation, does he generally destroy the land, people, or both?

Chapter 32

What I learned: The Egyptians had a preoccupation with the afterlife (as the pyramids were built to ensure the Pharaoh's comfort).

The question: Is what we know about heaven (as Christians) enough to understand the afterlife?

Chapter 33

What I learned: Some of us think that we have done enough good deeds to justify committing sins we don't want to give up.

The question: Why do people go to church? Do people really put the words they hear into practice, unlike the Israelites?

Chapter 34

What I learned: When our leaders fail us, we must not despair, but remember that God's in control and that he promises to return and care for his flock.

The question: How does people know if they are ready to play the role of God's good shepherd and lead other Christians?

Chapter 35

What I learned: As Edom received the judgment that it gave to destroy Jerusalem, we must also be careful not to pass judgment on others to avoid being judged.

The question: Is it more likely that there are countries that are enemies of Christians or more likely that people don't support Christian beliefs?

Chapter 36

What I learned: To regain sensitivity to certain sins, we must feel sorry for displeasing God, recognize our sin, and ask God for forgiveness.

The question: Why did God give the Israelites new hearts to protect his holy name at this time when he could have done so at any time?

Chapter 37

What I learned: The dry bones represented the people's spiritually dead condition.

The question: As God planned to put the two kingdoms of Israel together, why were these nations separated in the first place?

Chapter 38

What I learned: In this chapter, Ezekiel revealed how Israel (God's people) would be restored to their land from many parts of the world.

The question: Is there a definitive way to determine whether some messages in the Bible are symbolic or literal as well as when they occurred?

Chapter 39

What I learned: With God on our side, we are assured ultimate victory over our foes because God will fight on our behalf.

The question: When the Lord said, "You will eat flesh and drink blood" (verse 17) was he referring to the birds or the Israelites?

Chapter 40

What I learned: This chapter represents a vision intended to typify God's perfect plan—centrality of worship, presence of the Lord, its blessings, and the orderliness of worship.

The question: Why does the Bible include visions in such great detail that never happen in reality?

Chapter 41

What I learned: This chapter described the most holy place, which was the innermost room in the temple and where God's glory was said to dwell.

The question: Why is it important to know the dimensions (and their significance) of the whole temple?

Chapter 42

What I learned: Approaching our holy God must not be taken lightly in biblical times, shown when priests had to wear special clothes to minister in the temple.

The question: Is the design of the temple and its perfect symmetry a representation of the order and harmony in God's perfect kingdom?

Chapter 43

What I learned: If we do not understand the basic concept of holiness, we will never progress very far in our Christian faith.

The question: Were the Israelites seeking forgiveness but not completely ridding themselves of idolatry, causing postponement in building the temple?

Chapter 44

What I learned: Unbelievers weren't allowed to enter the temple.

The question: Are there biblical standards for those who work in the church as to who receives what portion of tithes given by the church?

Chapter 45

What I learned: As expected in today's society, God also asked the leaders (princes) to give up violence and oppression and do what was just and right.

The question: Is the amount and type of offerings given to God connected in any way to leadership position, or is it based solely on money and time?

Chapter 46

What I learned: God did allow for diversity in worship, but expected order and continuity.

The question: Did the Israelites find it challenging to give the different amounts and types of offerings that God required?

Chapter 47

What I learned: Even when we feel messed up and beyond hope, his power can heal us.

The question: Do foreigners represent those who are non-Christian?

Chapter 48

What I learned: The pressures of everyday life may persuade us to focus on the here and now and thus forget God.

The question: Does the "prince" (verse 21) described in this chapter represent Jesus?

BOOK TWENTY-SEVEN

Daniel

Chapter 1

What I learned: When Daniel resolved not to defile himself, he was being true to a lifelong determination to do what was right and not give in to pressures around him.

The question: Is our faith being tested during the times God allows his own work to suffer?

Chapter 2

What I learned: Before rushing to share the news about the dream, Daniel took time to give God credit for all wisdom and power and answering his request.

The question: What are things we can do to show how thankful we are for what God does for us?

Chapter 3

What I learned: Let us determine to be true to God no matter how difficult the pressure or punishment and not make excuses for not serving him.

The question: Would the average Christian be able to take the same stance for God like Shadrach, Meshach, and Abednego and risk death?

Chapter 4

What I learned: We may recognize that God exists and does wonderful miracles, but God is not going to change us until we acknowledge him as Lord.

The question: What were Nebuchadnezzar's actions of insanity when God showed the Israelites that God was in control through Nebuchadnezzar?

Chapter 5

What I learned: Archaeologists have discovered Belshazzar's name (an ancestor of Nebuchadnezzar) on several documents.

The question: Did Daniel accept the gift of being the third highest ruler in the kingdom (verse 29) although refusing originally (verse 17)?

Chapter 6

What I learned: Our prayers are usually not interrupted by threats but simply by the pressure of our schedules although God is our lifeline.

The question: Is praying three times a day the standard for the number of times we should pray?

Chapter 7

What I learned: All believers' names are written in the Book of Life, and they need not to fear judgment.

The question: Who is the person in verse 15 who interpreted Daniel's dream for him?

Chapter 8

What I learned: Daniel was appalled by this vision of world powers that dominated one another because it was beyond his understanding.

The question: What is the true meaning and significance of the second coming of Christ?

Chapter 9

What I learned: The Lord our God is merciful and forgiving even though we have rebelled against him, and we have not obeyed the law or kept the laws he gave us through his servants.

The question: Are natural disasters such as hurricanes and tornadoes likely a consequence of our disobedience?

Chapter 10

What I learned: Daniel mourned by eating no choice food, no meat or wine, and used no lotion because these were signs of feasting and rejoicing.

The question: What should Christians understand about supernatural powers, supernatural beings, and angels?

Chapter 11

What I learned: Due to the minimal information on the rivalries between the ancient kings and the connection to future events, this is one of the most complex chapters to understand.

The question: Are there other manuscripts that give information on the historic king listed in this chapter?

Chapter 12

What I learned: David was expected to spend the rest of his life in the comfort of God's sovereignty and look forward to the time when he would have eternal life with God.

The question: Why would Christians be fearful of death if the end times is when we receive great rewards for believing in God?

BOOK TWENTY-EIGHT

Hosea

Chapter 1
What I learned: Hosea was commanded to marry a woman who was unfaithful to him to show that the Northern Kingdom was unfaithful to God by worshiping other gods.

The question: Why did Hosea specifically choose Gomer as the promiscuous woman by which Hosea would have children?

Chapter 2
What I learned: There is no way for us by our own efforts to reach God's high standard for moral and spiritual life, but he graciously accepts us and forgives us.

The question: Can we always be aware when God has compassion on us and what actions are best to take to thank God for his compassion?

Chapter 3
What I learned: Hosea was commanded to buy back his adulterous, unrepentant wife and continue to love her and buy her gifts.

The question: Are there current behaviors that share similarities with idol worship?

Chapter 4
What I learned: The priests were glad when the people sinned because as people bought their sin offerings, the more the people sinned, the more the priests received.

The question: Do Christians find some connections with prosperity and televangelist preachers who make more money if they ask for more tithes?

Chapter 5

What I learned: Although leaders can impact whether we move away from God, God still holds us responsible for our own actions.

The question: What are sins for Christians that persist deep in their hearts? Why are these sins so deep?

Chapter 6

What I learned: A religious ritual is helpful only if it is carried out with an attitude of love for and obedience to God.

The question: Does God give special blessings to those who proclaim him to the world, as he said to the Israelites?

Chapter 7

What I learned: Without God's direction, our thoughts are filled with lust, cheating, selfishness, and deceit, which causes us to not reach our full potential.

The question: Does God handle intentional and unintentional sins differently?

Chapter 8

What I learned: We, like Israel, often call on God to ease our pain without wanting him to change our behavior, and we may repent after it is too late.

The question: How do we decide on the sacrifices we give? How do we know if God is pleased with our sacrifices?

Chapter 9

What I learned: We should still listen to messengers who speak to us through God who may tell us our approaches are all wrong, and consider viewpoints different from our own.

The question: How does sexual sin differ between current times and biblical times?

Chapter 10

What I learned: When we prosper, consider where the money is going and whether or not it is being used for God's purposes.

The question: Have we had presidents who put their belief in God when it came to winning wars without making alliances?

Chapter 11

What I learned: Look for hidden acts of nurturing, and notice those who make the world better through their love, but thank God first.

The question: What does it mean to seek to become like God knowing that becoming like him (or anywhere close) is impossible?

Chapter 12

What I learned: The two principles that Hosea called his nation to live by, love and justice, are at the very foundation of God's character.

The question: Are these the same principles that keep Christians away from the church (lack of love or too much justice [critique])?

Chapter 13

What I learned: For those who have trusted in Christ for deliverance from sin, death holds no threat of annihilation.

The question: When God indicated that the guilt of Ephraim was stored up and kept on record, did God choose not to forgive?

Chapter 14

What I learned: When our shortcoming and our awareness of our sins overcome us, we must remember that God's compassion never fails.

The question: Does God forgive in the same manner for those who do not believe in God?

BOOK TWENTY-NINE

Joel

Chapter 1

What I learned: God judges all people for their sins, but he is merciful to those who turn to him and offers them eternal salvation.

The question: What understanding do we have about the final judgment? Do Christians see the urgency to stop sinning and turn to God?

Chapter 2

What I learned: Through repentance to God, he promises to meet the deepest needs of those who love him by loving us, forgiving us, giving us purpose in life, and giving us a caring Christian community.

The question: Do we have a reason to fear because although we have asked for forgiveness, we still continue to sin?

Chapter 3

What I learned: Joel was trying to convince the people to wake up, get rid of complacency, and realize the danger of living apart from God.

The question: What should we understand about the geographic locations mentioned in the Bible?

BOOK THIRTY

Amos

Chapter 1

What I learned: Amos's message to believers is to work against injustices in society and to aid those who are less fortunate.

The question: Was God's great fury caused by idolatry, violence, and oppression of the poor in comparison to other sins?

Chapter 2

What I learned: God condemned Israel for (1) selling the poor as slaves, (2) exploiting the poor, (3) engaging in perverse sexual sins, (4) taking illegal collateral, and (5) worshipping false gods.

The question: Were any of the rich people in biblical times faithful followers of God? Were there poor people who were very corrupt?

Chapter 3

What I learned: The prophets gave the Israelites numerous warnings to turn from their sins; however, they received God's judgement for refusal to repent.

The question: Does God give preachers the knowledge to understand judgments such as natural disasters?

Chapter 4

What I learned: No matter how God warned the people—through famine, drought, blight, locusts, plague, or war—they still ignored him.

The question: What are examples when Christians ignore God?

Chapter 5

What I learned: God emphasizes the way we treat the poor because the poor can give us nothing, and how we treat them reflects our true character.

The question: How should Christians best go about giving to the poor? Is it better to give knowledge of money to the poor?

Chapter 6

What I learned: Some Israelites grossly wasted their resources for beds of ivory instead of using that money to help the poor due to their pride.

The question: How do we know if we as Christians are giving enough to help the poor?

Chapter 7

What I learned: Twice Amos was shown a vision of Israel's impending punishment, and his immediate response was to pray that Israel would be spared.

The question: Do preachers spend too much time on positive messages without much emphasis on the consequences of sin?

Chapter 8

What I learned: The merchants were keeping the religious festivals but not in spirit, because their ultimate goal was to make money.

The question: Why do people (especially Christians) turn to the Bible to address problems in their lives?

Chapter 9

What I learned: Going to church and being good is not enough, but we must believe in God so that it penetrates all area of our conduct.

The question: What are differences that we should know between Jews and Gentiles? Did God punish them differently based on their conduct?

Obadiah

Chapter 1

What I learned: Of all Judah and Israel's neighbors, Edom was the only one not promised any mercy from God because they rejoiced at the misfortunes of Israel and Judah.

The question: Are there current nations that are hostile to God like Edom?

Jonah

Chapter 1

What I learned: We have a great responsibility to obey God's Word because our sin and disobedience can hurt others around us, as Jonah's sin with the pagan sailors.

The question: Aren't we all guilty to some extent like Jonah in that there are certain violent places that we fear giving God's messages in?

Chapter 2

What I learned: When life is going well, we tend to take God for granted, but when we lose hope, we cry to God.

The question: Are we guilty of finding Bible passages such as Jonah being inside a fish for three days hard to believe?

Chapter 3

What I learned: If we proclaim what we know about God, we may be surprised to find that both atheists and those who are wicked may listen.

The question: Was there a way in which Jonah gave his message of being overthrown that got so many wicked people to listen?

Chapter 4

What I learned: Jonah was very angry at God and wanted to die because the very wicked Ninevites were being forgiven. Jonah was embarrassed.

The question: Is there ever a situation in which we can be angry with God since we deserve none of his mercy and compassion?

BOOK THIRTY-THREE

Micah

Chapter 1
What I learned: Two sins are identified in Micah's message—the perversion of worship and injustice toward others.

The question: Does God consider certain sins incurable in us through continuation, as was true of Samaria's sins?

Chapter 2
What I learned: Preachers are popular when they don't ask too much of us and only tell us what we want to hear.

The question: How often should clergymen speak to Christians about the consequences of our sins?

Chapter 3
What I learned: We, like the leaders of Jerusalem, should not treat God like a light switch to be turned on only as needed.

The question: Why do we have fear of speaking out on God's behalf on what is right?

Chapter 4
What I learned: A glimpse of God's plan for his followers should motivate us to serve him and change our sinful behavior.

The question: Since we do not know God's thoughts, does the Bible give us all necessary details about God's future plans?

Chapter 5
What I learned: Because of Christ's first coming, we have an opportunity to experience peace with God with no fear of judgment, and no more conflict and guilt.

The question: What are some of the similarities and differences between God and Jesus, and to whom do we make our prayers to?

Chapter 6

What I learned: God wants his people to be fair, just, merciful, and humble, which results in changed lives as opposed to just giving religious sacrifices.

The question: How much "religious" activity is necessary for us to live the life that God expects of us?

Chapter 7

What I learned: When we face trials because of our sin, we should not be angry with God or afraid that he has neglected us, but instead be patient and obedient.

The question: Does God put us through trials and tribulations for other reasons besides sin? How do we minimize such trials?

BOOK THIRTY-FOUR

Nahum

Chapter 1

What I learned: When people wonder why God doesn't punish evil immediately, remember that if he did, none of us would believe.

The question: Who is considered to be an enemy of God? Are there enemy nations in current times, such as Nineveh was?

Chapter 2

What I learned: There is a point for people, cities, and nations after which there is no return, and Assyria (Nineveh) had passed that point.

The question: Can we commit a sin so often that God does not forgive it and executes punishment for the sin?

Chapter 3

What I learned: No power on earth can protect us from God's judgment or be a suitable substitute for his power in our lives.

The question: Did those people in Nineveh really believe that God would destroy them? Were there any Christians who lived in Nineveh?

BOOK THIRTY-FIVE

Habakkuk

Chapter 1

What I learned: Injustice is still rampant, but we shouldn't let our concern cause us to doubt God or rebel against him, but instead we must recognize God's long-range plans.

The question: As we dig deeper into God's Word, does God reveal more answers to Habakkuk's complaints and to his long-range plans?

Chapter 2

What I learned: Living by faithfulness to God is helpful to all Christians who must live through difficult times without seeing signs of hope.

The question: How do we maximize our ability to be patient through difficult times?

Chapter 3

What I learned: We cannot see all that God is doing, and we cannot see all that God will do, which can give us confidence and hope in a confusing world.

The question: When we know that we are in a group that will be punished, should we do like Habakkuk and not pray for escape and accept the discipline?

BOOK THIRTY-SIX

Zephaniah

Chapter 1

What I learned: The Israelites were given numerous opportunities to change their behavior from idolatry and follow God, but they refused to change.

The question: Do we sin as Christians because we (like the Israelites) don't always believe that God will act and punish immediately?

Chapter 2

What I learned: "Seek righteousness, seek humility, perhaps you will be sheltered on the day of the Lord's anger" (verse 3) was the message to Judah and Jerusalem.

The question: How does the level of specific sins impact our ability to seek righteousness?

Chapter 3

What I learned: We need to gather together and pray, to walk humbly with God, to do what is right, and to hear the message of hope regarding the new world to come.

The question: Which of these sins most likely made God destroy Jerusalem (other than the remnant), idolatry or refusal to repent?

BOOK THIRTY-SEVEN

Haggai

Chapter 1

What I learned: When we hear a good sermon or lesson, we should ask what we should do about it, and then make plans to put it into practice.

The question: What actions do we see from Christians to determine that serving God is a high priority in their lives?

Chapter 2

What I learned: God wanted the temple to be rebuilt, and he had the gold and silver to do it, but he needed willing hands.

The question: How much time are we expected to give daily to do God's work?

BOOK THIRTY-EIGHT

Zechariah

Chapter 1

What I learned: Because God's Word endures, we must read, study, and apply what is preserved for us in Scripture so we will not have to repeat the mistakes of others.

The question: Why did God allow the pagan nations to afflict his people beyond his intentions?

Chapter 2

What I learned: A vast majority of the Israelites remained in Babylon (although they were warned that Babylon would be destroyed) because of perceived security.

The question: Does "Lord" refer to Jesus (Messiah), God, or both when the phrases in the Bible state "declares the Lord"?

Chapter 3

What I learned: We cannot remove our sins by our own effort, but we must allow them to be removed through Christ.

The question: Are the levels of grace, mercy, and forgiveness determined by our actions, or has God predetermined them for other reasons?

Chapter 4

What I learned: What we do for God may seem small and insignificant at the time, but God rejoices in what is right, not necessarily what is big.

The question: Why was the rebuilding of the temple not of the size and splendor of the temple built during King Solomon's reign?

Chapter 5

What I learned: When Christ died, he removed sin's power and penalty and gave us the power to overcome sin in our lives.

The question: What is the significance of using a woman to personify wickedness?

Chapter 6

What I learned: If we have unconfessed or habitual sin in our lives, confess it and turn away from it because confession releases God's mercy.

The question: In the visions of the four chariots, what is the significance of the red horses and no mention of any horses going east?

Chapter 7

What I learned: Any sin seems more natural the second time. Each repetition is easier.

The question: Can it be difficult for Christians to understand that God's ways are not our ways when he states, "When they called, I would not listen since they didn't" (verse 13)?

Chapter 8

What I learned: It was hard to believe that one day God himself would reign from Jerusalem and that their land would enjoy great peace and prosperity.

The question: As with the Israelites in building the temple, why is doing the work of God difficult to sustain for Christians?

Chapter 9

What I learned: God states in verse 8, "Never again will an oppressor overrun my people, for I am now keeping watch."

The question: What is meant by God's statement of "now I am keeping watch" (verse 8), as it seems to indicate that God wasn't watching before?

Chapter 10

What I learned: When we stay closely connected to God, the Spirit will enable us to do his will despite the obstacles.

The question: Why are different denominations of those who believe in God not united as God intends?

Chapter 11

What I learned: The thirty pieces of silver paid to the evil shepherd was the same amount Judas received for betraying Jesus (the price of a slave).

The question: Were there actually two or three shepherds in this passage, or was Zechariah just playing the role of these shepherds (favor and union)?

Chapter 12

What I learned: It is the Spirit who convicts us of sin, reveals to us God's righteousness and judgment, and helps us as we pray.

The question: Can we always understand when the Holy Spirit intervenes on our behalf?

Chapter 13

What I learned: The righteous remnant will be refined and purified, which may mean some trials and troubles at times.

The question: Was there any significance of the fractional remnant of the one-third that was left in the land?

Chapter 14

What I learned: Be ready for God's coming by studying his Scriptures carefully and making sure that we live as he intends— in obedience and spiritual readiness.

The question: What was so significant about the Festival of Tabernacles in biblical times? Is there a representation of this for Christians?

BOOK THIRTY-NINE

Malachi

Chapter 1
What I learned: If we give God only our leftover time, money, and energy, then this reflects the true attitude we have toward God.

The question: What are the differences between priests of the biblical times, priests of the current time, priests of current Jews and Catholics, and Christian preachers?

Chapter 2
What I learned: Loving God with all our heart, soul, and strength requires listening to what God says in his Word, and then preparing to do what he says.

The question: Since even the remnants who God did not destroy repented for their sins, does this mean that we will continue to sin and must ask for repentance?

Chapter 3
What I learned: When we give, we must remember that the blessings that God promises are not always material and may not be experienced here on earth.

The question: Does God values the types of tithes (money, goods, services) differently, as well as the meaning of "ten percent"?

Chapter 4
What I learned: We must be willing to accept God's refining process in our lives, which requires great sacrifice on our part.

The question: Is it expected that the refining process will be painful or result in some type of loss?

Matthew

Chapter 1

What I learned: The conception and birth of Jesus Christ are supernatural events beyond human logic or reasoning, so God sent angels to help with understanding.

The question: What should we understand about good and bad angels that impact the mission of Jesus?

Chapter 2

What I learned: Today, people are often afraid that Christ wants to take things away, when in reality, he wants to give us real freedom, peace, and joy.

The question: Who, in current times, represents the role of the magi in biblical times?

Chapter 3

What I learned: To be productive for God, we must obey his teaching, resist temptation, actively serve and help others, and share our faith.

The question: Can we fulfill God's requirement of confession of sin without baptism?

Chapter 4

What I learned: The devil's temptation focused on three major areas: physical needs and desires, (2) possession and power, and (3) pride. But Jesus did not give in.

The question: Why did God need to fast specifically for forty days and forty nights? How do we know when we should fast?

Chapter 5

What I learned: Jesus said that the desire to have sex with someone other than the spouse is mental adultery, so if the act is wrong, then so is its intention.

The question: Because lust and sex before marriage occurs so frequently, how do we separate mental adultery from natural attraction to the opposite sex?

Chapter 6

What I learned: All Christians struggle with temptation, so we must ask God to help us recognize temptation and give us the strength to overcome it.

The question: How do we decide when to save money for the future and when we should use money to build God's kingdom?

Chapter 7

What I learned: It is futile to try to teach holy concepts to people who don't want to listen and will only tear apart what we say.

The question: Are there forums around that allow believers and nonbelievers to discuss the existence of God and his principles?

Chapter 8

What I learned: Following Jesus is not always easy or comfortable, and often it means great cost and sacrifice, with no earthly rewards or security.

The question: Is sin considered an incurable disease because there will always be obstacles we face that will show our lack of faith?

Chapter 9

What I learned: When people look at God's law and compare themselves to it, they realize how far they fall short and how badly they need to repent.

The question: When we repent at a certain time, is it expected that we will have to repent again for the same sin?

Chapter 10

What I learned: We must find a balance between wisdom and vulnerability to accomplish God's work.

The question: What are the differences between Jews and Gentiles today? Are the expectations of Christ different?

Chapter 11

What I learned: Too often we justify our inconsistencies because listening to God may require us to change the way we live.

The question: Although the "yoke" (verse 29) between the Christian and God is shared, how do we put more of the yoke on Jesus to ease our difficulties?

Chapter 12

What I learned: The Pharisees had established thirty-nine categories of actions forbidden on the Sabbath based on interpretation of God's law on Jewish custom.

The question: Is the Sabbath still considered Sunday? Is working on the Sabbath (other than serving and worshipping God) considered a sin?

Chapter 13

What I learned: If we can't see God's work, perhaps it is because of our unbelief, so we must ask God for a mighty work in our lives.

The question: Should God's leaders also use parables when talking to Christians?

Chapter 14

What I learned: When we are apprehensive about the troubles around us and doubt Christ's ability to help, we must remember that he is the only one who can really help.

The question: How much time do Christian leaders spend in prayer alone with God? What are their recommendations for other believers?

Chapter 15

What I learned: For out of the heart comes evil thoughts—murder, adultery, sexual immorality, theft, false testimony, and slander—which defile a person.

The question: Is the practice of the *corbin* (dedicating money to God instead of parents) vow still made today?

Chapter 16

What I learned: The eternal destiny of Christians is secure, but Jesus will look at how they handle gifts, opportunities, and responsibilities in order to determine their heavenly rewards.

The question: Do we have to be in ministry to have the time to maximize understanding of Jesus and give nearly full commitment to him?

Chapter 17

What I learned: We shouldn't get upset at ourselves for being slow to understanding everything about Jesus, as even the disciples had difficulty understanding Jesus.

The question: How does God want us to show greater faith to others? What actions should Christians be doing?

Chapter 18

What I learned: For a Christian, any relationship, practice, or activity that causes us to sin should be stopped because it affects our minds and hearts.

The question: What is the role of angels watching over children and Christians? Are we ever expected to attempt communication with them?

Chapter 19

What I learned: A good reason to remain single is to use the time and freedom to serve God as some eunuchs (men without testicles).

The question: Is homosexual marriage and divorcing because of domestic violence considered sins today?

Chapter 20

What I learned: The blind beggars could see that Jesus was the Messiah, while the religious leaders who witnessed Jesus's miracles were blind to his identity.

The question: Is it appropriate to want the same level of forgiveness as someone else although it is not deserved?

Chapter 21

What I learned: To get our requests fulfilled, it must be in line with God's will, which is more likely with strong belief and faith in God.

The question: What type of religious groups do we have in the current day that represent the Pharisees?

Chapter 22

What I learned: Jesus said that if we truly love God and our neighbor, then we naturally keep the other commandments.

The question: How much time should we invest in talking to those who try to get us (or others) to not believe in the existence of Jesus?

Chapter 23

What I learned: Serving keeps us aware of others' needs, and it stops us from focusing on ourselves.

The question: Do Christians have any representation of phylacteries (boxes containing Scriptures)? Is this equivalent to the caps worn by Jews?

Chapter 24

What I learned: Only a solid foundation of God's Word can equip us to perceive the errors and distortions in false teaching.

The question: In preparation for Christ's return, should more time be spent on studying God's Word or sharing God's Word with others?

Chapter 25

What I learned: What we do for others demonstrates what we really think Jesus's words mean to us, such as feed the hungry, help the homeless, and tend to the sick.

The question: Does God prescribe specific methods on how we should go about feeding the hungry, helping the homeless, and tending to the sick?

Chapter 26

What I learned: The way to overcome temptation is to be aware of the possibilities of temptation be sensitive to the subtleties and being spiritually equipped to fight temptation.

The question: Since Jesus was in great anguish over his approaching physical pain, is it expected that we will be fearful when we know we will suffer?

Chapter 27

What I learned: The disciples who publicly followed Jesus had fled, but a Jewish leader, Joseph of Arimathea, secretly followed Jesus and asked to bury his body.

The question: Once Jesus died and the barrier between God and humanity was removed, do priests now have the same role as bishops, pastors, and so on?

Chapter 28

What I learned: Baptism symbolizes submissions to Christ, a willingness to live God's way, and identification with God's covenant people.

The question: Are there people who believe in the existence of Jesus and not the resurrection? Why is the resurrection difficult to believe?

BOOK TWO

Mark

Chapter 1

What I learned: Determine to pray more on a regular basis, not just in times of crisis, as even Jesus had to set aside time to prayer.

The question: Do demons still take control of people? Is demon possession something that can be recognized?

Chapter 2

What I learned: Fasting empties the body of food, and repentance empties the life of sin, but fasting must be done with the right motives.

The question: What are some of the key differences and practices between Judaism and Christianity?

Chapter 3

What I learned: We should not disqualify ourselves from service to Christ because we do not have the expected credentials since service to Jesus requires only a willing heart.

The question: Are spirits able to talk because of some acquired human qualities?

Chapter 4

What I learned: Our witness may be weak, and our efforts may seem to influence so few, but the Word of God is a powerful growth agent.

The question: Are there defined stages of spiritual growth? What factors play the biggest role in advancing to the highest stages (stronger relationship with God)?

Chapter 5

What I learned: Some people, usually women, made mourning a profession and were paid by the dead person's family to weep over the body.

The question: Is it the concepts of the supernatural that occur throughout the Bible that make the words of the Bible difficult to believe for both Christians and non-Christians?

Chapter 6

What I learned: As we work to bring wholeness to people's lives, we must never ignore the fact that all of us have both physical and spiritual needs.

The question: Are there other reasons beside faith in God's ability as to why we don't pray for what seems impossible?

Chapter 7

What I learned: An evil action begins with a single thought and allowing our minds to dwell on lust, envy, hatred, or revenge, which then leads to sin.

The question: Is it expected that we will have these evil thoughts? Can any person be expected to be free of these evil thoughts?

Chapter 8

What I learned: Jesus told the disciples not to tell anyone about them because they needed more instruction about what Jesus would accomplish through death and resurrection.

The question: Do Christians have difficulty talking about the Bible to others because they don't really understand what is being said?

Chapter 9

What I learned: It was natural for the disciples to be confused about Jesus's death and resurrection because they could not see into the future.

The question: Why was the transformation of Jesus (verses 2–4) necessary for us to know, and wasn't his divine nature shown through his miracles?

Chapter 10

What I learned: It is easy to say we will endure anything for Christ, yet most of us complain over the most minor problems.

The question: Is divorce a sin unless the divorce occurs for permissible reasons as stated in the Bible?

Chapter 11

What I learned: For effective prayer, we must (1) be a believer, (2) not hold a grudge against another person, (3) not pray with selfish motives, and (4) pray for the good of God's kingdom.

The question: Does the Bible give any information on whether we should pray more about our needs, the needs of others, or prayers of thanks?

Chapter 12

What I learned: We need not be afraid of eternal life because of the unknowns, but concentrate on our relationship with Christ right now.

The question: Are people afraid of death more because of what is unknown or the pain that often accompanies death?

Chapter 13

What I learned: We don't have to be fearful or defensive about our faith because the Holy Spirit will be present to give us the right words to say.

The question: How much concern should Christians place on the end times and Jesus's return when the future is unpredictable?

Chapter 14

What I learned: To resist temptation, (1) keep watch, (2) pray to God, (3) have the support of friends and loved ones, and (4) focus on God's purpose for our life.

The question: Why did Jesus have to suffer so painfully when he died for our sins?

Chapter 15

What I learned: Joseph, a secret disciple of Christ and an honored member of the Sanhedrin, took Jesus's body for burial so that the resurrection could be confirmed.

The question: Is it natural to deny Jesus to minimize any significant pain and suffering, which makes it hard to understand the pain Jesus offered for us?

Chapter 16

What I learned: We share a commonality with Pilate who allowed Jesus's crucifixion under pressure although he believed God was innocent, in that we know what is right and do what is wrong.

The question: What is the significance (as it relates to belief) as to verses 9–20 not being included in early manuscripts?

BOOK THREE

Luke

Chapter 1

What I learned: Zechariah and Elizabeth had been childless for many years and were too old to expect any change in their situation.

The question: How do we develop understanding between waiting for a blessing and recognizing that God may not answer a prayer?

Chapter 2

What I learned: When we do God's will, we are not guaranteed comfort and convenience.

The question: Because several people in the Bible doubted God, does this mean that they had a lack of faith? Is this considered a sin?

Chapter 3

What I learned: Like Jesus, we need to resist the temptation to jump ahead before receiving the Spirit's direction and wait for God's timing.

The question: Are we truly repentant of the sins that we repeat? What are those sins that Christians commit repeatedly?

Chapter 4

What I learned: Many people sin by attempting to fulfill legitimate desires outside of God's will or ahead of his timetable.

The question: What are examples of demon possession today? How does it relate to demon possession in biblical times?

Chapter 5

What I learned: When Simon Peter didn't believe God regarding the catching of the fish, he says, "Go away from me, Lord; I am a sinful man"(verse 8)!

The question: Is it more detrimental to not recognize our sin or to recognize our sin and continue sinning?

Chapter 6

What I learned: When life is calm, our foundation of knowing Jesus may not seem to matter, but when crises come, our foundations are tested.

The question: What specific actions should we engage in to show others that we want to strengthen our foundation?

Chapter 7

What I learned: The Pharisees and religious leaders wanted to live their own way by justifying their own point of view and refused to listen to other ideas.

The question: Who was the sinful woman who anointed Jesus's feet? Did she commit a specific sin (because she lived "a sinful life") (verse 37)?

Chapter 8

What I learned: Our witness for Christ should be public, and we should seek opportunities to shine our light unbelievers need help to see.

The question: How do we best help those "thorn patch" people (those who are overcome by worries and materialism but leave no room and time in their lives for God?

Chapter 9

What I learned: Real faith is built on three cornerstones, the Law (Moses), the Prophets (Elijah), and Jesus.

The question: How do we measure peoples' ability to minister to the people of Jesus as he expects of us?

Chapter 10

What I learned: God wants Christians to pray, recruit, and equip others to come together as they explore opportunities to serve Jesus.

The question: When the messengers were sent ahead of Jesus to heal the sick, did the people primarily listen to the gospel because of the healings?

Chapter 11

What I learned: Three aspects of prayer in God teaching the disciples how to pray is its content, our persistence, and God's faithfulness.

The question: How do we help nonbelievers and believers accurately interpret Scripture and not have it distorted as the Pharisees did in biblical times?

Chapter 12

What I learned: Many non-Christians use the supposed (or real) hypocrisy of Christians as an excuse to stay away from God and the church.

The question: How do we balance saving money in retirement versus giving money to others in need?

Chapter 13

What I learned: Whether a person is killed in a tragic accident or miraculously survives is not a measure of righteousness, as Jesus does not address this.

The question: Can much of our fear that we have be due to the unknown and the matter in which we die?

Chapter 14

What I learned: Many Christians blend into the world and avoid the cost of standing up for Christ.

The question: What actions should Christians maintain to show an unswerving commitment to Christ's kingdom?

Chapter 15

What I learned: If we are refusing to forgive people, we are missing a wonderful opportunity to experience joy and share it with others.

The question: Are we guilty of not risking helping specific groups of people, unlike Jesus?

Chapter 16

What I learned: Most religious leaders of Jesus's day permitted a man to divorce his wife for almost any reason, but God considers this adultery.

The question: How do we discern when to say "no" to opportunities to give money to people in need?

Chapter 17

What I learned: Those who live for themselves display these common attitudes: materialism, individualism, and skepticism.

The question: Should we expect additional blessings from God for being obedient?

Chapter 18

What I learned: Jesus wants his people to enjoy prayer by delighting in his company, find ways to read the Bible, seek God, rely on him, and trust him explicitly.

The question: How are the beggars of biblical times different than the homeless of current times as it relates to changing their lives?

Chapter 19

What I learned: In every society, certain groups of people are considered "untouchable" because of political views, immoral behavior, and lifestyle.

The question: What is the significance of Palm Sunday? What should Christians do with the palms and their representation?

Chapter 20

What I learned: We must not think of heaven as an extension of life as we now know it because this life is limited by time, death, and sin.

The question: Is there a religion currently that supports the view of the Sadducees who only support the Pentateuch and don't believe in the resurrection?

Chapter 21

What I learned: It is abnormal to want to suffer, but as Jesus's followers, we are willing to suffer if, by doing so, we can build God's kingdom.

The question: Since most don't give all they have to live on like the widow, have we "missed the mark" because we gave a percentage out of convenience?

Chapter 22

What I learned: We need to be aware of our breaking points and not become overconfident and self-sufficient.

The question: If some suffering is put on us for building God's kingdom and doing his will, isn't it natural to pray for an end of suffering?

Chapter 23

What I learned: As believers, we may feel that we can't do much for Jesus, but we should model the women followers of Jesus who did the best they could.

The question: What are the similarities and differences between the criminal justice system that unfairly accused Jesus and the current one that unfairly treats people?

Chapter 24

What I learned: The resurrection of Jesus is the central fact of Christian history, but people will need time to comprehend it.

The question: When we die, do we also rise from the dead and perform some actions as Jesus did when he rose from the dead?

BOOK FOUR

John

Chapter 1

What I learned: "Truly I tell you, among those born of women there has not risen anyone greater than John the Baptist, yet whoever is the least of heaven" (Matthew 11:11).

The question: When John preached to people, did he preach primarily to believers or nonbelievers, and which should be emphasized more?

Chapter 2

What I learned: Those who believe in Jesus but run into situations they cannot understand must continue to trust that he will work in the best way.

The question: When Jesus attended the wedding where he turned water into wine, did Jesus expect sin when he indicated that the guests would have too much to drink?

Chapter 3

What I learned: No matter how intelligent or well educated we are, we must come to Jesus with an open mind and heart so he can teach the truth about God.

The question: Does God send the Holy Spirit only through Baptism? How do people know that the Holy Spirit is in them?

Chapter 4

What I learned: We are nourished not only by what we take in, but also by what we give out for God.

The question: What are the primary differences between Jews, Christians, and Catholics as it relates to delivering God's Word?

Chapter 5

What I learned: The Pharisees and the religious leaders believed in God, but created rules in the Old Testament to trap Jesus because they did not believe him.

The question: Can we accept Jesus as our Savior (beginning of eternal life), and then no longer accept Jesus and be condemned to hell?

Chapter 6

What I learned: We are united with Christ by believing in his death and resurrection and by devoting ourselves to living as he requires and depending on his teaching.

The question: As we need to eat every day (with variety), should our prayer life be equivalent to maintain a right relationship with God?

Chapter 7

What I learned: Although many people talk about Christ in church, when it comes to making a public statement about their faith, some are often embarrassed or fearful.

The question: Are we concerned about talking about Jesus publicly to avoid confrontation and being defined as "judgmental" by non-Christians?

Chapter 8

What I learned: In several places in the Bible, Jesus intentionally welcomed those who wanted to question his claims and character if people followed through on their discoveries.

The question: As Christians, are we always comfortable having discussions about Jesus since our understanding may be limited?

Chapter 9

What I learned: When we suffer from a disease, tragedy, or a disability, we must try not to ask, "What did I do wrong?" but instead ask God for a clearer perspective on what is happening.

The question: Can it be difficult to explain suffering and the loss of innocent lives to non-Christians when even Christians can't explain it?

Chapter 10

What I learned: There are many reasons to be afraid on earth because this is the devil's domain; however, following Jesus will give us everlasting safety.

The question: Do we have similar celebrations to the Feast of Tabernacles and the Feast of Dedication?

Chapter 11

What I learned: Jesus allowed Lazarus to die so that Jesus's power over death could be shown to his disciples and others.

The question: Do we share the same feelings as Mary and Martha since we can't really explain the timing of when our loved ones die?

Chapter 12

What I learned: Many Jewish leaders wouldn't admit to faith in Jesus because they feared excommunication from the synagogue (which was their livelihood).

The question: What are the challenges people face in reaching out to Christ in the general public?

Chapter 13

What I learned: Jesus knows exactly what we will do to hurt him, but he still loves us unconditionally and will forgive us whenever we ask for it.

The question: How do we strengthen attributes of loving based on Jesus's sacrificial love such as giving until it hurts and devoting energy to the welfare of others?

Chapter 14

What I learned: Sin, fear, uncertainty, doubt, and numerous other forces are at war within us, but the peace of God in our hearts offers comfort in place of conflict.

The question: How do we become more aware of the Holy Spirit's activities? How do we define the Holy Spirit?

Chapter 15

What I learned: We may not have to show sacrificial love by dying for someone as Jesus did, but other ways of practicing sacrificial love include listening, helping, encouraging, and giving.

The question: What does God expect us to do specifically when Jesus says, "Go and bear fruit—fruit that will last" (verse 16)?

Chapter 16

What I learned: Three important tasks of the Holy Spirit are: (1) conviction of sin and repentance, (2) revealing the standard of righteousness to believers, and (3) demonstrating Christ's judgment over Satan.

The question: If all believers are priests when Jesus died for us, allowing us to talk to God directly, why do Catholic parishes still have priests?

Chapter 17

What I learned: This chapter is Jesus's prayer to God, which discusses the forces of Satan's power and those under God's authority are at war.

The question: Why does Jesus state, "I am not praying for those of the world, but those you have given me" (verse 9), as opposed to praying for all people?

Chapter 18

What I learned: Pilate knew that Jesus was innocent, but caved in to the public pressure and the potential loss of his job and illegally had Jesus executed.

The question: Do we share similarities with Pilate when we don't speak about Jesus due to the work environment or outside conflict?

Chapter 19

What I learned: During crucifixions, accusers had been suffocated quickly by breaking their legs so that they would not be able to push up with their legs to breathe.

The question: When Jesus says that "the one who handed me over to you is guilty of a greater sin" (verse 11), does that give value to sin and indicate that some religious leaders will go to hell?

Chapter 20

What I learned: We can doubt without living a doubting way of life because doubt can encourage thinking and sharpen the mind.

The question: How is doubt (possible positive behavior) different that lack of faith (a perceived negative behavior)?

Chapter 21

What I learned: We may be uncertain and fearful about our future, but if we know God is in control, we can confidently follow Christ.

The question: When Jesus asks Peter, "Do you love me? Do you really love me? Are you even my friend?" what actions show a "yes" to these questions?

BOOK FIVE

Acts

Chapter 1
What I learned: God has important work for us to do for him, but we must do it by the power of the Holy Spirit.

The question: How do we know when we are ready to transition from a disciple (follower or learner) to an apostle (messenger or missionary)?

Chapter 2
What I learned: Some Jews still went to the temples and synagogues and would not separate from the Jewish community because they didn't believe Jesus was the Messiah.

The question: What religious group represents those who believe in God, but not in Jesus and the resurrection, and how can we change their views?

Chapter 3
What I learned: Many people want the benefits of being identified with Christ without admitting their own disobedience and turning from sin.

The question: Does God expect us to turn away completely from all sin, or does God expect sins, and then expect repentance?

Chapter 4
What I learned: When Peter and John prayed, they didn't ask God to remove the problem, but instead prayed for the strength and courage to deal with the problem.

The question: How do we speak boldly about God through talking to people directly without those people feeling judged?

Chapter 5

What I learned: Ananias and his wife Sapphira died immediately after questioning for lying to God and his people by keeping money that they received for the land.

The question: Did Ananias and Sapphira have an opportunity to ask for forgiveness of their sins before they were put to death?

Chapter 6

What I learned: If we are not in leadership, we have gifts that can be used by God in various areas of the church's ministry.

The question: How did the Twelve determine that the seven men who chose to distribute food were full of faith and the Holy Spirit?

Chapter 7

What I learned: Stephen was stoned to death for speaking the truth about the Israelites persecuting prophets and exposing their disobedience.

The question: Does God expect all Christians to speak courageously about him even if it results in persecution, or are only a select few trained to speak like this?

Chapter 8

What I learned: When we share the gospel, we should start where the other person's concerns are focused, and then show how God's Word applies to those concerns.

The question: How can we determine what portions of Old Testament Scripture are no longer relevant due to the change in times and the arrival of Jesus?

Chapter 9

What I learned: Saul (Paul), who was a persecutor of Christians, had to address the issue of whether Gentile believers had to obey Jewish laws before becoming Christians.

The question: If those people in biblical times did not see the many miracles of the apostles such as raising the dead, would they have still converted to Christianity?

Chapter 10

What I learned: Cornelius (Gentile) needed Peter (Jew) to know the way to salvation, and Peter needed Cornelius to know that Gentiles were included in God's plans.

The question: Should non-Jewish Christians attempt to learn about Jewish traditions to be more knowledgeable about Christianity?

Chapter 11

What I learned: It is significant that Antioch was the first place where believers were called Christians because all they had in common was belief in Christ.

The question: Were the churches in Antioch more representative of the nondenominational churches of today?

Chapter 12

What I learned: We cannot possibly answer why some die (James) and some are saved (Peter) in this life because we cannot see all that God sees.

The question: What can we understand about the role of God's angels (divinely created beings with supernatural powers) like the one who saved Peter?

Chapter 13

What I learned: It might be important at the time to point out someone's shortcomings, but before we do this, we must build that person's trust through encouragement.

The question: If true obedience to God requires risk, is it a sin when we don't take a risk to help others due to fear of confrontation?

Chapter 14

What I learned: Paul and Barnabas were persistent in their preaching of the good news, considering the costs and hardships to be nothing in comparison with obedience to Christ.

The question: How much of an impact did the stoning have on Paul in how he continued his preaching moving forward?

Chapter 15

What I learned: The three Christian positions were: Gentiles must be Jewish for salvation, faith in Christ is the only requirement for salvation, and faith is the only requirement with evidence of a changed lifestyle.

The question: Can a person be defined as a Christian if the person has not been baptized or circumcised, but only states belief in Jesus Christ?

Chapter 16

What I learned: Timothy volunteered to be circumcised to overcome any barriers to his witness for Christ because sometimes we need to go beyond the minimum requirements to help our audience.

The question: Was writing letters the only method of communication between the far-ranging ministries regarding unity and consistency between churches?

Chapter 17

What I learned: When witnessing to others, we should work with what we know, but we should always want to know more in order to reach more people and answer questions effectively.

The question: What did Paul mean when he says, "God overlooked such ignorance, but now he commands all people everywhere to repent" (verse 30)?

Chapter 18

What I learned: Luke, who was a doctor, historian, and historian of the books of Luke and Acts, showed excellence by how hard he worked as Paul's companion when no one was watching.

The question: Do we have missionaries today who can dedicate their entire lives by spreading the gospel and moving from place to place like Paul?

Chapter 19

What I learned: John's baptism (the original teaching method of the preacher Apollos) was a sign of repentance from sin (Old Testament), not a sign of new life in Christ.

The question: How do we know if we have an evil spirit in us? How does this evil spirit come out from within us?

Chapter 20

What I learned: Although Paul preached his messages in different ways to fit different audiences, his message remained the same, which was to turn away from sin and turn to Christ by faith.

The question: How do we measure how much work we are doing for God and determine if we are doing enough to serve him?

Chapter 21

What I learned: When we really want to do God's will, we must accept all that comes with it—even the pain.

The question: Should non-Jew Christians (Gentiles) have an understanding of Jewish laws? What laws do Jewish people have that Gentiles do not have?

Chapter 22

What I learned: When we witness to Christ, we must first identity ourselves with the audience, then they will much more likely listen if they feel a common bond with us.

The question: Do Christians simply choose not to minister to others because they are not likely to listen anyway?

Chapter 23

What I learned: God's ways are not our ways, and we should not limit God by asking him to respond our way.

The question: Is it common for family to disown people for becoming Christians, as was possible with Paul's family?

Chapter 24

What I learned: Few things test our patience and faith like being forced to wait, which perhaps explains why God puts us in situations where we have no other choice but to wait.

The question: Why did Paul have to defend himself while the Jewish leaders accusing Paul of rioting, running a cult, and desecrating the temple had a lawyer (Tertullus)?

Chapter 25

What I learned: Rather than complaining about our present situations, look for ways to use every opportunity to serve God and share knowledge of God with others.

The question: What impact does the religious beliefs of our leaders in the political realm have on the direction of our country?

Chapter 26

What I learned: We still have eyewitnesses accounts of Jesus's life recorded in the Bible, as well as historical and archeological records of the early church to study.

The question: How do we get a burning desire (like Paul) to see others come to Christ? What skills do we need?

Chapter 27

What I learned: It is wrong to sit and do nothing about our situations when we can take actions to fix our problems.

The question: Did God expect all those in the boat to be completely absent of fear and pray to God for protection?

Chapter 28

What I learned: The book of Acts deals with the history of the Christian church and its expansion in ever-widening circles touching influential critics in the Western world.

The question: How do we both spread the gospel and change lives and behaviors for those who accept the message?

BOOK SIX

Romans

Chapter 1

What I learned: Sexual desires are of such importance that the Bible gives them special attention because it requires more self-control than any other desire.

The question: Does God allow natural disasters and disease to kill innocent children to address the wickedness of people and those who choose not to follow God's laws?

Chapter 2

What I learned: We have all sinned repeatedly, and there is no way apart from Christ to be saved from sin's consequences.

The question: Does witnessing to others and asking them to change their behavior offer challenges because we sin ourselves and people feel that they are being judged?

Chapter 3

What I learned: No amount of human achievement or progress in personal development will close the gap between God's moral perfection and our imperfect daily performance.

The question: Since the following of the law does not give us eternal life, does following the law allow God to be pleased and give us blessings on earth?

Chapter 4

What I learned: Faith is believing and trusting in Jesus Christ and reaching out to accept his wonderful gift of salvation.

The question: How is our faith in God impacted when we don't trust ourselves or don't believe God will answer us because of previous sins?

Chapter 5

What I learned: The law was added to help people see their sinfulness, to show us the seriousness of our offenses, and to drive us to God for mercy and pardon.

The question: Although God has died for our sins, how does the type of sin we commit and how often it is repeated impact our separation from God?

Chapter 6

What I learned: To minimize sin, we can (1) identify our personal weaknesses, (2) recognize what tempts us, (3) avoid temptation, (4) practice self-restraint, (5) use time wisely, and (6) lean on God.

The question: Do Christians fear death itself, or do Christians fear the pain and suffering that often take place prior to death?

Chapter 7

What I learned: The great tension in our daily Christian experience is the conflict that we agree with God's commands but cannot do them (painful awareness of sin).

The question: Is it likely that people who keep the rules, laws, and customs of Christianity love God although these things do not save us but expose our sin?

Chapter 8

What I learned: If we have sincerely trusted Christ for our salvation and acknowledged him as Lord, then the Holy Spirit has come into our lives, and we are Christians.

The question: What is meant by the verse, "We do not know what we ought to pray for, but the Spirit himself intercedes for us through wordless groans" (verse 26)?

Chapter 9

What I learned: The fallacy of gaining salvation by human effort remains in that people still think good intentions are the key to unlock the door of eternal life.

The question: What are the relationships between doing Christian work for God, faith, blessings, mercy from God, and eternal life?

Chapter 10

What I learned: There should never be a debate between those who favor lifestyle evangelism (living proclaims the gospel) and confrontation evangelism (declaring the gospel), but they should coincide.

The question: How do we give constructive advice to those who do not follow the law and its consequences when we also do not always follow the law?

Chapter 11

What I learned: Paul had a vision of a church where all Jewish and Gentile believers were united in their love of God and in obedience to Christ.

The question: What are the primary differences between members of Jewish synagogues, nondenominational churches, Baptist churches, and AME churches?

Chapter 12

What I learned: When we identify our own gifts, we should ask how we can use them to build God's family.

The question: How does the church evaluate the gifts of its members? How does administration decide how the gifts can contribute to the church?

Chapter 13

What I learned: Some Christians believe that the government is so corrupt that we should be good citizens, but that we should not vote, work in the government, or serve in the military.

The question: What are the beliefs of those who make the final decisions on the laws that we must follow? Do they consider biblical principles?

Chapter 14

What I learned: Through sharing ideas, we can come to a fuller understanding of what the Bible teaches through accepting, listening, and respecting the opinion of others.

The question: How do we get Christians to strengthen their faith without those people feeling judged?

Chapter 15

What I learned: We should read our Bibles diligently to increase our trust that God's will is best for us.

The question: Can we ever be satisfied with the work that we do to serve others and the time we invest to strengthen our faith?

Chapter 16

What I learned: Priscilla and Aquila ministered effectively behind the scenes as missionaries and used their home for church meetings.

The question: Do all Christians have to play some role in missionary work to effectively build God's kingdom?

BOOK SEVEN

1 Corinthians

Chapter 1

What I learned: We can spend a lifetime accumulating human wisdom and yet never learn to have a personal relationship with God.

The question: How do we determine if people give enough time to obtain a strong relationship with God and help others strengthen their faith?

Chapter 2

What I learned: Spiritual discernment allows us to (1) use God's perspective to draw conclusions, (2) make wise decisions, (3) recognize God's spirit, (4) correctly use Scripture, and (5) identify false teachers.

The question: Can we increase our spiritual discernment more by talking about Christ with others or studying the Bible?

Chapter 3

What I learned: Only nonbelievers should fear death because Christ has conquered all fears for believers, and they know that death is the beginning of eternal life with God.

The question: How should "weak" Christians begin to build a stronger foundation on Jesus Christ?

Chapter 4

What I learned: It is tempting to judge fellow Christians, evaluating if they are good followers of Christ, but only God should judge because he knows the heart.

The question: How do Christians differentiate between pointing out sins to people and being judgmental?

Chapter 5

What I learned: Paul does not expect anyone to be sinless because all believers struggle with sin daily.

The question: Should we judge those Christians who blatantly sin and not those non-Christians who sin, according to verse 12?

Chapter 6

What I learned: Those who say that they are Christians but persist in evil practices with no sign of remorse will not inherit the kingdom of God.

The question: Why is sexual immorality (sex outside the marriage, lust) so difficult to control and not viewed by society as problematic?

Chapter 7

What I learned: Sexual pressure is not the best motive for getting married, but it is better to marry the right person than to "burn with passion" (verse 9).

The question: How can people withhold all natural sexual desires (kissing, touching, and so on) and never lust and remain unmarried as Paul suggests?

Chapter 8

What I learned: Some actions may be perfectly acceptable for us to do, however, but may harm a Christian brother or sister still young in the faith.

The question: Is eating meat considered sinful or unacceptable to some Christians today?

Chapter 9

What I learned: Self-discipline requires an honest look at our strengths and weaknesses and learning attitudes that do not come naturally to serve God's purposes.

The question: What role does being a paid employee or a volunteer employee have when meeting the needs of the church and serving God?

Chapter 10

What I learned: Paul gave strong encouragement to the Corinthians about temptation, which was: (1) wrong desires and temptations happen to everyone, and (2) others have resisted temptation.

The question: How do Christians teach about matters that lead weaker Christians to leave the faith, but are not forbidden in Scripture?

Chapter 11

What I learned: Paul indicates that believers should look and behave in ways that are honorable with their own culture.

The question: If the Lord's Supper is of importance for Christians, why is communion not held during Sunday service at all churches?

Chapter 12

What I learned: Too often, the up-front gifts, like speaking or teaching, are more highly regarded than the behind-the-scenes gifts, like helping and serving.

The question: How can the church survey the church members to find out their God-given gifts?

Chapter 13

What I learned: Faith is the foundation and content of God's message, hope is the attitude and focus, and love is action that keeps faith and hope in line.

The question: What are the differences when we use "love" in the context of loving strangers, loving family members, and loving God?

Chapter 14

What I learned: Tongues, then, are a sign not for believers but for unbelievers; prophecy, however, is not for unbelievers but for believers; but speaking in tongues is a gift.

The question: When people show that they are "in the spirit" or speaking in tongues in churches today, should this be done in private since it can't be interpreted?

Chapter 15

What I learned: Belief in the resurrection will affect our view of the future because Christians know that life continues beyond the grave, which will never end.

The question: Why do we fight through trying to keep our physical bodies on earth when our heavenly bodies will be perfect, and we will live through eternal life free of pain?

Chapter 16

What I learned: Paul told the Corinthians to (1) be on their guard, (2) stand firm, (3) be courageous, (4) be strong, and (5) do everything in love.

The question: How do we get the mind-set of Paul where he has no fear of losing his physical body and would sacrifice his life for Christ?

BOOK EIGHT

2 Corinthians

Chapter 1

What I learned: Suffering should be thought of as the necessary pain that accompanies spiritual growth because it helps produce perseverance and Christian character.

The question: If suffering has so many benefits in strengthening our faith and Christian character, why do we pray to avoid it?

Chapter 2

What I learned: Paul thanked God for his ministry, his relationship with the Corinthian believers, and the way God used him to use others despite difficulties.

The question: How do Christians decide when they should charge (making a profit) for doing the work of God?

Chapter 3

What I learned: When we trust Christ to save us, he removes our heavy burden of trying to please him and our guilt for failing to do so.

The question: Since keeping the Old and New Testament laws do not save us, should we emphasize some Old Testament laws that no longer apply?

Chapter 4

What I learned: Knowing that we will live forever with God in a place without sin and suffering can help us live above the pain we face in this life.

The question: Could we make the case that we cannot handle the suffering and opposition because God doesn't equip us with such spiritual strength?

Chapter 5

What I learned: Facing the unknown may cause anxiety and leaving loved ones hurts deeply, but if we believe, we will have eternal life with Christ.

The question: As Christ's ambassadors, how do we determine if we (or others) are doing enough to know what changes are necessary to do more for God?

Chapter 6

What I learned: Don't let our careless or undisciplined actions be another person's excuse for rejecting Christ.

The question: What forms of entertainment will likely cause us to sin or allow nonbelievers to influence our behaviors?

Chapter 7

What I learned: A mature Christian should graciously accept constructive criticism, sincerely evaluate it, and grow from it.

The question: Does the Bible give any information about the two lost letters by Paul, how they got lost, and what was contained in these letters?

Chapter 8

What I learned: Most believers would not want their faith in God, knowledge, or love of God to stop at a certain level, but we may tithe at a fixed percentage for life.

The question: How do Christians decide if they should increase their giving to the church or increase how much they save for themselves each year?

Chapter 9

What I learned: People may hesitate to give generously to God if they worry about having enough money left over to meet their needs.

The question: Although "how" we give is more important than the "amount" we give, can we model "how" to give since this is difficult to see and evaluate?

Chapter 10

What I learned: When exposed to ideas and opportunities that lead to wrong desires, we can recognize the dangers and turn away or allow unhealthy thoughts to take us captive.

The question: How do we determine the timing and effort we invest in defending the gospel when positions conflict with biblical teaching?

Chapter 11

What I learned: Keeping Christ first in our life can be very difficult when we have so many distractions threatening to sidetrack our faith.

The question: How do you sacrifice your life for the gospel as Paul had done?

Chapter 12

What I learned: Three times Paul prayed for healing of a chronic and debilitating problem but did not receive the healing, but rather received gifts far greater from God.

The question: How is our faith in God affected when we pray for healing, do not receive it, and cannot understand God's refusal?

Chapter 13

What I learned: Paul called the Corinthians to examine and test themselves to see if they really were Christians.

The question: Can people change from being Christian to non-Christian if people admit to no longer believing in God? How does God respond?

BOOK NINE

Galatians

Chapter 1

What I learned: Some people assert that all religions are equally valid ways to God when God asserts that the only way to him is through faith in Jesus Christ.

The question: Do Jewish people still believe that to be saved people must follow the Jewish traditions and follow the rules of Moses along with faith in Christ?

Chapter 2

What I learned: The law (1) guards us from sin by giving us standards of behavior, (2) convicts us of sin, and (3) drives us to trust in the sufficiency of Christ, but does not save us.

The question: When Paul preached and wrote his letters to the Corinthians, how did he know if they understood his messages?

Chapter 3

What I learned: In the Old Testament, there were three categories of laws: ceremonial (Israel's worship), civil (daily living), and moral (direct commands by God).

The question: Is it clear in Scripture which laws we are no longer bound (as Paul indicates) to follow in the Old Testament?

Chapter 4

What I learned: Christians are those who believe inwardly and outwardly that Jesus's death has allowed God to offer them forgiveness and eternal life as a gift.

The question: What are the different "types" of Christians? What are the similarities and differences related to the law and being saved by faith in God?

Chapter 5

What I learned: "The acts of the flesh are obvious: sexual immorality, impurity, debauchery, hatred, jealousy, fits of rage, selfish ambitions, dissensions, factions and envy, drunkenness, orgies, and the like" (verses 19 and 20).

The question: What are the decisions behind circumcisions of children? Does God expect Christians to be circumcised?

Chapter 6

What I learned: It is discouraging to continue to do right and receive no word of thanks or see no tangible results, but in due time, we will reap a harvest of blessings.

The question: Should we put more emphasis on some laws than others? Does God emphasize laws that have greater effects on the majority of Christians?

BOOK TEN

Ephesians

Chapter 1

What I learned: As Christians, we can be confident that God has won the final victory and is in control of everything, and we need not fear any dictator, nation, death, or Satan.

The question: If the best methods to improve our relationship with God are through studying the Word of God and prayer, are there guidelines to the amount of time for prayer and study time?

Chapter 2

What I learned: While no action or work we can do can help us obtain salvation, God's intention is that our salvation will result in acts of service.

The question: When we serve others, should we decide how to serve based on our gifts, or should we invest more time in serving Christians or non-Christians?

Chapter 3

What I learned: God calls us to follow him, which means willingness to endure pain so that God's salvation can reach the entire world.

The question: Since we don't naturally want to face pain, is our level of commitment to Christ and his mission linked to our pain tolerance and sacrifice?

Chapter 4

What I learned: Although we have a new nature, we don't automatically think all good thoughts and express all the right attitudes when we become new in Christ.

The question: What is the difference between committing sins and "living in sin"? Do we address these situations differently when we help others get closer to God?

Chapter 5

What I learned: "But among you there should not be even a hint of sexual immorality among you because it is improper for God's holy people" (verse 3).

The question: Is the husband's submission to God different than the wife's submission to the husband? What is meant by the word "submit" in Scripture?

Chapter 6

What I learned: A method of constant prayer is to make brief and quick prayers our habitual response to situations that we meet throughout the day.

The question: When we pray and our prayers do not get answered, is it due to more to Satan's power over us or our lack of faith?

BOOK ELEVEN

Philippians

Chapter 1

What I learned: If we're not ready to die, then we're not ready to live, so we must make certain of our eternal destiny, then we will be free to serve without fear of death.

The question: As Paul is also in conflict between living in the body and living with Christ, don't we work harder to live in the body now than living with Christ?

Chapter 2

What I learned: Paul observed that most believers are too preoccupied with their own needs to spend time working with Christ.

The question: How does the church decide how much time should be devoted by Christians as it relates to mission work, helping the church, and studying the Bible?

Chapter 3

What I learned: No amount of law keeping, self-improvement, discipline, or religious effort can make us right with God, but only trusting in Christ.

The question: What should we be doing here on earth that will prepare us for the next life? Do we do little because we don't know enough about heaven?

Chapter 4

What I learned: Paul's advice about not being anxious about anything is to turn our worries to prayers.

The question: Because Paul has learned to be content regardless of his circumstances, should we pray for more opportunities for being content?

BOOK TWELVE

Colossians

Chapter 1

What I learned: Because Christ is the sustainer of all life, none of us are independent of him, and we must trust him for protecting us, caring for us, and sustaining us.

The question: Is it difficult to understand that Jesus is God since Jesus is visible, God is invisible, and Jesus is also called the Son of God?

Chapter 2

What I learned: Following a long list of religious rules requires strong self-discipline and morality, but religious rules cannot change a person's heart.

The question: Should we invest more time in understanding contrary biblical beliefs such as Gnosticism and changing the viewpoints of these groups?

Chapter 3

What I learned: We must consider ourselves dead and unresponsive to sexual immorality, impurity, lust, evil desires, and greed, keeping in mind that we must stand before God.

The question: Can we rid ourselves of God's wrath and judgment if we ask for forgiveness when we sin?

Chapter 4

What I learned: Faith shouldn't die if the answers come slowly, for the delay may be God's way of working his will in our lives.

The question: What are the reasons why prayers for healing or prayers to accomplish certain tasks are delayed or currently not answered?

BOOK THIRTEEN

1 Thessalonians

Chapter 1

What I learned: We can feel as though God deserted us or God couldn't stop our suffering, but because we live in a sinful world, believers will suffer.

The question: What does it mean when Christ comes back (second coming)? How can we react appropriately when we don't understand it?

Chapter 2

What I learned: Many of the difficulties that prevent us from accomplishing God's work can be attributed to Satan.

The question: Because Satan is real, what should Christians understand about Satan and how he may cause to sin in our actions and thoughts?

Chapter 3

What I learned: Some think that troubles are always caused by sin or lack of faith, but trials may be a part of God's plan since persecution can build character.

The question: When trials and tribulations happen to us, can they always be explained?

Chapter 4

What I learned: All Christians, including those living when Christ returns, will live with Christ forever, so we need not fear death for ourselves or our loved ones.

The question: When death is believed to be near, should we hope for it to come soon to be with God, or fight hard and pray for healing?

Chapter 5

What I learned: A prayerful attitude is built around our dependence on God, realizing his presence within us and obeying him fully.

The question: Since evil doesn't come from God and God controls the world, does God allow evil to occur because of sinful behavior and changing mind-sets?

BOOK FOURTEEN

2 Thessalonians

Chapter 1
What I learned: The keys to surviving persecution and trials are perseverance and faith, understanding that God is fair and will use our trials for our good and his glory.

The question: If we have not suffered much, could this be due to our faith in God and God's grace, or has the time not come yet to endure suffering?

Chapter 2
What I learned: We don't need to understand every detail of how God works in order to have perfect confidence in his absolute power over evil and his total goodness toward us.

The question: What should we know about the antichrist and the man of lawlessness? How do they impact us today?

Chapter 3
What I learned: In chapter 1, we are told what suffering can do for us; in chapter 2, we are assured of final victory; and in chapter 3, we are told to live responsibly despite difficult trials.

The question: How do we properly balance leisure, laziness, and doing the work for Christ?

BOOK FIFTEEN

1 Timothy

Chapter 1
What I learned: Arguing about details of the Bible can send us off on interesting (but irrelevant) tangents and can cause us to miss the intent of God's message.

The question: What are some of the false teachings (and teachers) of today's time? Are these teachings intentional or unintentional?

Chapter 2
What I learned: In first-century Jewish culture, women were not allowed to study, but Paul allowed them to learn with an attitude of quietness and composure (not total silence).

The question: How does a church discern if someone has enough biblical knowledge and maturity in the faith to become a leader in the church?

Chapter 3
What I learned: New believers should have a place of service, but they should not be placed in leadership positions until they are firmly grounded and have knowledge in the Word of God.

The question: Does the meaning of "new believer" represent the time that we believe in God or the amount of biblical knowledge that we have?

Chapter 4
What I learned: Failing to use our talents can waste away from lack of practice.

The question: What is the most common false teaching that convinces people not to develop a relationship with God today?

Chapter 5

What I learned: Take the initiative and look for a way to serve those who have no family or who are elderly, young, disabled, ill, or poverty-stricken with their needs.

The question: How does the church respond to those who ask for help but are lazy and will not work?

Chapter 6

What I learned: Christianity is an active religion that requires active faith, training, working hard, sacrificing, and doing what we know is right.

The question: How hard should Christians work to become rich if money is the root of all kinds of evil (playing the lottery)?

BOOK SIXTEEN

2 Timothy

Chapter 1

What I learned: Paul promised Timothy that God would give him strength and that he would be ready when it was his turn to suffer.

The question: When God informs us that our life here on earth will be ending soon, what does God expect from us on our final days?

Chapter 2

What I learned: The truth that Jesus is one person with two united natures has never been easy to understand and has been debated by false teachers, but that doesn't make it untrue.

The question: How do we have productive discussions as Christians about topics in which we may disagree, such as tithing and the representation of Scripture?

Chapter 3

What I learned: Everyone who wants to live a godly life in Christ Jesus will be persecuted, while evildoers and impostors will go from bad to worse, deceiving and being deceived.

The question: How does immediate gratification (pleasure) move us to sin or to not believe in God's message?

Chapter 4

What I learned: It is our responsibility to do all we can to keep the gospel message alive for the next generation.

The question: What specific knowledge and what evidence do we need to provide to the next generation to show how to live for God and spread the gospel?

BOOK SEVENTEEN

Titus

Chapter 1

What I learned: We will not know for certain in this life those who claim to know God, but a glance at their lifestyles will quickly tell us what they value and if they have kingdom priorities.

The question: Which of these aspects of living is most difficult for Christians: faith, knowledge of the truth, or living in godliness?

Chapter 2

What I learned: Both living and waiting are essential to our Christian sanity in this present evil age, but the living is made bearable by seeking to build God's kingdom.

The question: How do men best improve their self-control to set an example for younger men? What are examples of loss of self-control?

Chapter 3

What I learned: "But avoid foolish controversies and genealogies and arguments and quarrels about the law, because these are unprofitable and useless" (verse 9).

The question: What are some of the foolish controversies that take place between "active" Christians and "non-active" Christians?

BOOK EIGHTEEN

Philemon

Chapter 1

What I learned: When God finds runaways (such as the slave Onesimus), he often sends them back to the very places and people from which they ran from in the first place.

The question: Although Paul requested that Onesimus be forgiven and viewed as a Christian brother instead of a slave, did Philemon actually forgive Onesimus when he returned?

BOOK NINETEEN

Hebrews

Chapter 1

What I learned: Angels are God's messengers—spiritual beings created by God and who serve specific functions such as serving believers, protecting the helpless, claiming God's messages, and executing God's judgment.

The question: Did Jesus speak in the Old Testament since he worked with God who created the world?

Chapter 2

What I learned: When we belong to God, we need not fear death because death is not the end but the only doorway into eternal life.

The question: Can we truly understand the suffering of others (or our own suffering) and why God decided that we should suffer (especially the end of this life)?

Chapter 3

What I learned: To prevent having an unbelieving heart, we should stay in fellowship with other believers, talk daily about our faith, be aware of deceitfulness of sin, and encourage each other with love.

The question: Should we invest more time in understanding the Bible, helping others, or trying to improve ourselves through Godly behavior?

Chapter 4

What I learned: The demands of God's Word require decisions, and we must not only listen to the Word (on Sundays), but we must also let it shape our lives.

The question: How do we determine if we have peace (Sabbath rest) with God?

Chapter 5

What I learned: "In fact, though by this time you ought to be teachers, you need someone to teach you the elementary truths of God's Word all over again" (verse 12).

The question: Other than the Bible, where do we turn or who do we turn to in order to gain a stronger understanding of interpreting Scripture in today's context?

Chapter 6

What I learned: Basic beliefs include the importance of faith, the foolishness of trying to be saved by good deeds, the meaning of baptism and spiritual gifts, and the facts of resurrection and eternal life.

The question: How can churches use Sunday services to assess knowledge of the basics and beyond? What are the consequences of a lack of understanding?

Chapter 7

What I learned: Because of the sacrificial system (sacrificing animals), the Israelites were aware that sin costs something and that they themselves were sinful.

The question: Why do we pray for God to forgive our sins if our past, present, and future sins were forgiven when Jesus died for us?

Chapter 8

What I learned: If our hearts are not changed, following God's rules will be unpleasant and difficult, and we will rebel against being told how to live.

The question: Could we determine if people follow aspects of the old covenant (external rules) but not the new covenant (faith and heart toward God)?

Chapter 9

What I learned: If we are carrying a load of guilt because we are finding that we can't be good enough for God, we need to take another look at Jesus's death and what it means to us.

The question: Does the concept of animal sacrifice for sins make sense for people currently since we aren't always punished immediately for committing sin?

Chapter 10

What I learned: God's new way for us to please him is not by keeping laws or even abstaining from sin, it is by coming to him in faith to be forgiven, and then following him in loving obedience.

The question: What is the relationship between living in faith and committing sins (does one have a direct effect on the other)?

Chapter 11

What I learned: "Now faith is the confidence in what we hope for and assurance about what we do not see, so we must leave work for the unexplainable works of God" (verse 1).

The question: Should we expect to receive blessings in this life? Can we comprehend what blessings will look like in the next life?

Chapter 12

What I learned: If we have a secret weight such as pornography, gambling, or alcohol, we must admit our need and get help today.

The question: Is there a direct correlation between the level of suffering and how often we sin and the types of sins we commit?

Chapter 13

What I learned: Praise God early in the day before morning rush, then again in the hurried middle, and at the end of the business day.

The question: As the writer of Hebrews recognizes the need of prayer, what should we pray about, and how much time should be invested in prayer?

BOOK TWENTY

James

Chapter 1

What I learned: God allows Satan to tempt people in order to refine their faith and to help them grow in the dependence in Christ.

The question: What are some of the reasons why our prayers are not answered?

Chapter 2

What I learned: We cannot earn our salvation by serving and obeying God, but such actions show that our commitment to God is real.

The question: How do we know if people have true faith in God? Can peoples' level of faith be measured through actions (works)?

Chapter 3

What I learned: Jesus warns that although it is good to aspire to teach, teachers' responsibility is great because their words affect others' spiritual lives.

The question: Because of the impact of evil the tongue can have, when is it best not to speak at all or not to give a response?

Chapter 4

What I learned: We tend to think that doing wrong is sin, but James tells us that sin is also not doing right (sins of commission and sins of omission).

The question: Is it selfish to primarily pray to God to satisfy personal needs and goals and spend less time praying for those we do not know personally?

Chapter 5

What I learned: Christians disagree on whether or not people can lose their salvation, but agree that those who leave the faith need to repent.

The question: How do we determine if people have left the faith or have backslidden?

BOOK TWENTY-ONE

1 Peter

Chapter 1

What I learned: Instead of saying, "Why me?" when facing trials, we should respond with confidence that God knows, perseverance when facing trials, and courage not to be afraid.

The question: If people only face a minimal amount of trials, does this mean that they had great faith in God?

Chapter 2

What I learned: Christ died for our sins, in our place, so that we would not have to suffer the punishment we deserve, which is called substitutionary atonement.

The question: Other than prayer, what actions do we need to take to prepare ourselves for suffering?

Chapter 3

What I learned: While some Bible passages such as "the reaching of the imprisoned spirits" (verse 19) may be unclear, we can discover certain truths from them along with the context of the rest of Scripture.

The question: Is baptism a requirement to become a Christian? Does it make sense to be baptized more than once if we have backslidden or lost belief in God?

Chapter 4

What I learned: Some people, well aware of their abilities, believe they have the right to use them as they please, while others believe they have no special talent at all.

The question: Although suffering helps us be like Christ, isn't it natural to try to avoid pain?

Chapter 5

What I learned: It takes humility, however, to recognize that God cares, to admit our need, and to let others in God's family help us.

The question: Do we live in an evil world because the world is being ruled by Satan? Is God allowing this?

BOOK TWENTY-TWO

2 Peter

Chapter 1

What I learned: Many believers want an abundance of God's grace and peace, but they are unwilling to put forth the effort to know him better through Bible study and prayer.

The question: Does God prepare us for the type of death we will face (as he did with Peter), or can we request to God the type of death we will face?

Chapter 2

What I learned: Many in our world today mock the supernatural and deny the reality of the spiritual world and claim that only what can be seen or felt is real.

The question: How do we refute the false teachings about the supernatural and spiritual world when the ideas behind them are not fully clear to us?

Chapter 3

What I learned: No matter where we are in our spiritual journey and no matter how mature we are in our faith, the sinful world always will challenge our faith.

The question: What should we emphasize to people about God's second coming and turning to God's ways before it is too late?

BOOK TWENTY-THREE

1 John

Chapter 1
What I learned: Admitting our sins means we (1) agree with God that our sin is a sin, and we are willing to turn from it; (2) ensure that we don't conceal our sins; (3) and recognize our tendency to sin.

The question: Other than our sinful nature, why do we sin repeatedly when we know the consequences of our sins?

Chapter 2
What I learned: Worldliness is internal because of (1) lust of the flesh, (2) lust of the eyes (materialism), and (3) the pride of being obsessed with status or importance.

The question: Is it possible that people go to church as a long-standing habit but never stopped to ask themselves why they do it and simply claim they are Christians?

Chapter 3
What I learned: We all have areas of weaknesses where temptation is strong and habits are hard to conquer, so we must deal with our areas of vulnerability.

The question: How do we measure Christians' ability to "love your brother and sister" when almost all people have some aspects of love in their character?

Chapter 4
What I learned: A particularly widespread false teaching called Docetism holds that Jesus is a spirit who only appeared to have a body.

The question: Can we say that we love God if we don't sacrifice any time or money on God's behalf?

Chapter 5

What I learned: When we communicate with God, we don't demand what we want, but discuss with him what he wants for us.

The question: Although we are guaranteed eternal life as Christians, why do we fear death and sometimes become angry? Do we understand the meaning of eternal life?

BOOK TWENTY-FOUR

2 John

Chapter 1

What I learned: We can show love by avoiding prejudice and discrimination, accepting people, and also by listening, helping, giving, serving, and refusing to judge.

The question: How do we go about confronting those false teachers? How do we decide the best time (if there is a time at all) to confront them?

3 John

Chapter 1

What I learned: Because of our individualistic, self-centered society, many lonely people wonder if anyone cares whether they live or die.

The question: Has the concept of hospitality changed from biblical times due to concerns of safety?

Jude

Chapter 1

What I learned: We contend for the faith by (1) studying the Bible, (2) growing personally with Christ, and (3) remaining unified on the basics of our faith.

The question: How can we prove the truth to those people who believe that what is stated in the Bible (especially the Old Testament) is no longer applicable today?

BOOK TWENTY-SEVEN

Revelation

Chapter 1

What I learned: The book of Revelation is complex and apocalyptic and is revealed to John in a vision that John attempts to describe using mysterious imagery and illustrations.

The question: Is the complexity of Revelation and the different approaches to interpret Revelation the primary reason why most sermons aren't given from Revelation?

Chapter 2

What I learned: It is popular to be open-minded toward many types of sin, calling them personal choices or alternative lifestyles.

The question: Is it challenging to stand up and rebuke sins that we may have once committed without being called "judgmental"?

Chapter 3

What I learned: We can minimize God's discipline by drawing near to him through confession, service, worship, and studying God's Word.

The question: How would we define a "lukewarm" Christian? What does the role of money and "peace of mind" have on this issue?

Chapter 4

What I learned: God's attributes are symbolized here as majesty and power (lion), faithfulness (ox), intelligence (man), and sovereignty (the eagle).

The question: How do we emphasize the importance of worship for those Christians who do not attend church services?

Chapter 5

What I learned: When we realize the glorious future that awaits us in heaven, we will find the strength to face our present difficulties.

The question: What should we understand about angels (good and bad angels)? What affect do they have on our lives?

Chapter 6

What I learned: The four riders represent God's judgment on people's sin and rebellion, but the riders are only given power over one-fourth of the earth, indicating that God is limiting judgment.

The question: Can this chapter be used to explain the acts of nature and violence by nonbelievers that occur in the world?

Chapter 7

What I learned: God seals his believers either by withdrawing them from the earth (Rapture) or by giving them special strength and courage to make through prosecution.

The question: Is there any significance in the one thousand sealed from each tribe in the 144,000?

Chapter 8

What I learned: The trumpet blasts have three purposes: (1) to warn that judgment is certain, (2) to call the forces of good and evil into battle, and (3) to announce the return of Jesus.

The question: When reading Revelation, how do we know which events already happened and which stated events only have symbolic meaning?

Chapter 9

What I learned: Evil spirits are ruled by Satan (not created by Satan) and are fallen angels who joined Satan's rebellion but are limited in power by God.

The question: Does God want to torture all those who don't believe in him or only those who don't believe in him and engage in evil acts?

Chapter 10

What I learned: We should want Christ to come because of the triumph of his kingdom, not because things are bad or because we want out of our struggles.

The question: Would people have a hard time believing that the judgments will take place for unbelievers if they currently are not suffering?

Chapter 11

What I learned: Obedience and immediate award are not always linked because this would mean good people would always be rich and suffering would always result in sin.

The question: When seven thousand people were killed in the earthquake, were some of them believers of God, or do they only represent evildoers or nonbelievers?

Chapter 12

What I learned: One of the reasons God allows Satan to work evil and bring temptation is so that those who pretend to be Christ's true believers will be weeded out.

The question: Did the war that took place in heaven between God and Satan result in Satan's evil fallen angels?

Chapter 13

What I learned: The number "666" symbolizes the worldwide dominion and evil of the unholy trinity (Satan, the Beast of the sea, and the Beast of the earth) to undo Christ's work.

The question: How do Christians attempt to minimize the physical persecution that we will face, while at the same time speaking out against Satan (and his followers)?

Chapter 14

What I learned: The secret to enduring is to trust God to give patience through the small trials we face daily and obey God even when obedience is unattractive or dangerous.

The question: Should Christians directly confront atheist and other devil-worshiping organizations about the judgment that they will face?

Chapter 15

What I learned: Our eternal reign with Christ won't begin until all evil is destroyed by his judgment.

The question: Do Christians believe that all evil will be destroyed while we are currently alive since Satan controls our world?

Chapter 16

What I learned: We must avoid the misconception that God must be fair and kind in dealing with humanity because God sets his own standard even if we don't understand it.

The question: How do we know when to give up on explaining these judgments to those who will not turn to God?

Chapter 17

What I learned: Although God allows evil to permeate this present world, the new Earth will never know sin.

The question: What is the most effective method to serve others and help those being persecuted for their faith?

Chapter 18

What I learned: We are to live according to the values Christ exemplified: service, giving, self-obedience, and truth.

The question: When we give to help others financially, is it better to tithe, give the money to charity, or give directly to those in need?

Chapter 19

What I learned: In each generation, there must be balanced preaching and teaching about God's grace and anger against sin.

The question: Why is the preaching of God's wrath and God's anger against sin not emphasized in church services?

Chapter 20

What I learned: The one thousand years is referred to as the millennium and the three major positions on the issue are post-millennialism, premillennialism, and amillennialism.

The question: Because the millennium and the resurrections (first and second) can be interpreted differently, should we simply take the view of our servant leader (pastor, bishop, and so on)?

Chapter 21

What I learned: To follow Christ requires boldness and bravery to stand for him when oppression occurs, so we must pray for courage to do what is right regardless of circumstances.

The question: Should we be curious about what happens to us when we leave the old earth and enter the new earth as described in this chapter?

Chapter 22

What I learned: In a world of problems, persecutions, evil, and immorality, Christ calls us to endure in our faith.

The question: Can we understand concepts such as "the time is near for God's return" or "I am coming soon" (verse 12), since his second coming is unknown?

www.ingramcontent.com/pod-product-compliance
Lightning Source LLC
Chambersburg PA
CBHW061423040426
42450CB00007B/882